Anthropology and Education

2 of

Anthropology and Education

Clara K. Nicholson

Department of
Anthropology
Utica College

Foundations of Education
Series

Charles E. Merrill Publishing Company, Columbus, Ohio
A Bell & Howell Company

Merrill's Foundations of Education Series under the editorship of
Dr. Ray C. Phillips, Auburn University, and Dr. Robert J. Stalcup, The Education Commission of the States.

Library of Congress Catalog Card Number: 68-12814

1 2 3 4 5 6 7 8 9 10—76 75 74 73 72 71 70 69 68

PRINTED IN THE UNITED STATES OF AMERICA

Foreword

Students of the educational scene today often note the existence of strong national concern for improving the quality of education and a renewal of the historic American commitment to equalizing educational opportunities for all children and youth. Improved preparation of school personnel is a parallel, though less obvious, concern. These concerns have provided the stimulus for more rapid and more substantial improvements in education in recent years than have been achieved in any previous generation.

As might be expected, programs of preparation for professional careers in education are currently the subject of careful study, inasmuch as improving education is partially a function of improved personnel. One of the most important ways of viewing programs for preparing professional educators is two-dimensional, basic or foundational preparation and specialized preparation. The former can be conveniently defined, although perhaps the definition is an oversimplification, as being made up of content appropriate to all professional educators while the latter is that preparation which is designed to prepare a person for a particular responsibility in the profession, for example, a first-grade teacher, or a high school biology teacher, or a school superintendent. Neither dimension of preparation is adequate alone. The foundations area provides needed professional perspective, knowledge of the cultural orientation of schools, philosophical directions of education, knowledge of human growth and development, learning theory, the primary methodology of teaching, and evaluation of learning outcomes. Specialization is preparation for discharging the responsibilities inherent in the particular position one holds in the educational system.

As is true of preparation programs for other major professions, those for professional educators make use of content from several disciplines. Such content is organized according to the purposes to be served by the particular program and requires adaptations to these purposes. As implied above, preparation for careers in education relies on the disciplines of philosophy, educational psychology, sociology, anthropology, and others for its content, as well as on the discipline of education. The subject matter selected from these supporting disciplines and applied to teacher education makes up the area of professional preparation known as the Foundations of Education. Such subject matter must take form in a meaningful pattern with interrelationships of the content from the respective disciplines made clear. When this occurs, a set of useful generalizations about education, its goals, its setting, its characteristics, effective teaching and the proper evaluation of learning is possible. These generalizations are critical in the development of a professional educator and without them only educational technicians are possible.

The *Foundations of Education Series* edited by Dr. Ray C. Phillips and Dr. Robert J. Stalcup properly emphasizes this important dimension of teacher education. There is a definite and important place in professional literature for this series. It should add much to the further professionalization of preparation for careers in education.

Truman M. Pierce, Dean
School of Education
Auburn University
Auburn, Alabama

Preface

This publication, like the others in this series, is designed to give the student of professional education an overview of a specific area within the professional education field.

Keeping up with the tremendous amount of writing published each year in the field of education poses, in itself, a virtually impossible task. For this reason the authors have felt a strong need to provide students with a capsule presentation of some of the basic concepts included in the major areas of study in professional education.

The use of this series of works should serve to give the student direction in carrying on more extensive study in those areas in which he is weak. The selective bibliography included in each of these publications should provide a point of departure for any additional investigation which the student feels is necessary. In any event the authors take the position that these publications represent the minimum information which any student of education needs to have.

R. C. Phillips
R. J. Stalcup
Editors

Table of Contents

Chapter 1

Introduction

Anthropology is the study of our favorite subject: ourselves. More precisely stated, anthropology derives from the Greek word *anthropos* meaning, "man," and *logos*, usually translated "study," thus, "man-study." Education is the process by which "selves" are shaped. One aspect of anthropological inquiry is the study of behavior which individuals learn and transmit, consciously or unconsciously. The anthropologist analyzes how this process shapes and molds the learner, the process of education.

Man's behavior is studied from so many aspects that it is fair to ask how the anthropological approach differs from other studies —how can anthropology contribute to education? In brief, the anthropologists compare the likenesses and differences among men. Traditionally, this investigation has centered on extant nonliterate peoples. Increasingly, however, theory and research methods developed and tested in the field are applied to modern communities and machine-using societies.

At the same time, anthropologists search earlier ages for an even broader perspective. Anthropologists who specialize in physical anthropology and archaeology probe the past million and a half years to discover the manner of man's adaptation to his physical and cultural environment. They trace continuity of cultural development in a search for trustworthy generalizations about man and his behavior. They describe the responses man has made in diverse situations throughout the world, and throughout time. Hunting and food-gathering people, agriculturists and herders, sea-going and machine age men, people in subsistence economies and lands of plenty have been faced with certain problems common to all men. Each, believing his solution to be "right" and "good," has made it part of his cultural base. Each respective way of life continues as these customs are transmitted, more or less intact, to each oncoming generation, and as these newcomers grow into persons like their forebears.

Anthropologists are concerned with all of man's behavior; his attempts to earn a living, maintain order and regulate behavior, cope with the unknown, find aesthetic and recreational expression, care for and rear the young, and transmit his cultural heritage. This review of the relations of anthropology and education is concerned with the last named activities: namely, rearing and caring for the young and transmitting culture. In these areas, the anthropologist can distribute to education a cross-cultural understanding of human behavior as well as a knowledge of the nature of culture.

The peoples of the world have found limitless ways of solving myriads of problems. It cannot be assumed, of course, that solutions found workable in one situation necessarily apply in another. Nevertheless, these wide vistas of behavioral possibilities can initiate a new perspective on human life and an increasing awareness of man's adaptive potential.

Insight into the nature of culture sensitizes an educator to cultural influences on his own and his students' behavior. Education itself is unquestionably a cultural process. It is the instrument by which cultures survive and develop. What is learned varies with each society and usually differs among groups within the same society. Different traditions foster unique and characteristic patterns of learning. In each instance, however, each new member is prepared, explicitly or implicitly, to cope more or less adequately with his cultural heritage. Although the learning situations vary, in all societies education is crucial to the cultural mode of life.

Culture has never remained static, although some periods and some societies in man's history have known more stability than others. Our society is not one of the latter, for our rapidly changing culture base and our cultural pluralism compound the problem. Integration of our society is increasingly difficult as sub-cultures present divergent values to the current generation, and the value of much of todays' culture for an unpredictable future comes under examination. The skill of educators and the effectiveness of their methods are taxed with a mounting difficulty of selection and an increasingly complex problem of presenting our burgeoning cultural repertory.

Anthropologists seek answers to four crucial questions about this study of human cultural accumulation, past and present. What is presented? Who presents it? Who learns it? What is learned? The first question draws on content presentation or transmission—behavioral prescriptives and alternatives, values and cultural traits, complexes and patterns. Answers to the second question are sought in the credentialing process. That is to say, what individuals have the *right* to present certain types of behavior? The third question leads into biological and social eligibility requirements for participation in various aspects of the education process, while the last question is approached from the learner's point of view. Answers are sought in the area of *Culture and Personality*.

The answers to these questions, although incomplete, can be applied wisely and effectively in the effort to preserve and enrich our way of life. At the same time, the anthropological understanding of the processes involved in learning a cultural tradition (enculturation), and of modification of one culture as it comes in more or less continuous contact with another (acculturation) may help us take advantage of the new opportunities industrialization affords. While we seek ways to cope with change, we hope to retain the values and more durable traditions of our rich heritage. This discussion seeks to present the anthropological point of view for your consideration.

Chapter 2

Historical Background

Although the myths and folklore of nearly all peoples indicate a fairly universal interest in others' behavior, it was not until around the fifteenth century that a storehouse of facts about "foreigners" began to accumulate. During this great age of exploration and discovery, travelers, missionaries and traders contributed a mounting assemblage of data. Some observations were accurate descriptions of the way people lived in other parts of the world, while others were tales exaggerated out of all proportion— "good for the telling" in a local pub or coffee house.

Most observers, however, were not objective, for they interpreted observed behavior in the light of their own standards. In most instances, the non-European was considered inferior. An impetus was given to these earlier pre-anthropological interests by the discovery in Europe early in the 19th century of skeletal remains and flint tools. These discoveries, however, would have failed to add much to the young science of anthropology, had it not been for the advancing knowledge of other sciences. By this

date, geological and paleontological researches were indicating
that the earth was much older than had been previously assumed.
Geologists established the fact that man had lived in Europe during
the last Ice Age.

A French scholar digging on the continent uncovered objects
proving that man lived and used stone tools well back in time.
The Englishman Lord Avebury, bent on a search of man's past,
uncovered artifacts, and established a distinction between Old
Stone Age (Paleolithic) and New Stone Age (Neolithic) cultures.
Further proof of man's antiquity came with the discovery in 1856
of the remains of a skeleton, now termed Neanderthal, a sub-
species of homo-sapiens. Thus techniques from related sciences
and accumulating evidence from the past added to the new science
of man—anthropology.

Although the chronological and spatial information on man and
his works was growing, much was left still to be learned. Nevertheless, on the basis of the available data, early scholars made attempts to classify man and to describe his position in the animal
world. One such attempt was made by Linnaeus in 1750. He
categorized man into four major groups: European whites, American reds, African blacks, and Asiatic yellows. By 1850, a comparative science of culture was being developed, and early anthropologists saw their discipline mainly as a natural science concerned
with non-Europeans, contemporary non-literate, and prehistoric
peoples. Chief among this group were E. B. Tyler of England,
whose major work *Primitive Culture* was published in 1865, and
L. H. Morgan in the United States, whose *Ancient Society* was
published in 1877. Modern anthropology began in the United
States near the turn of the 20th century, stimulated and colored
by the presence of our so-called "aboriginies" who had been ever
and usually violently before us.

In addition to the early comparative school, often termed "evolutionism," several other approaches developed as scholars undertook to organize cultural data. Historicalism, diffusionism,
functionalism (which gave birth to a precocious child—configura-
tionalism), and various social "interactional" schools succeeded
each other through the years. Although this labeling of "schools"
tends to over-simplify complex idea systems of many scholars,
perhaps the need for brevity justifies the action.

Although each theoretical method had certain intrinsic weaknesses, limiting the student's over-all view of man and his behavior, each in turn introduced new insight into the central problem. Some of these concepts, refined and redefined in the light of our ever-increasing knowledge of "man" are today useful and productive tools in the hands of competent anthropologists, for anthropology has reached maturity.

Evolutionism

The evolutionists tried to establish laws of a world-wide cultural progression. By 1860, their thinking was posited in a framework inspired by the Darwinian concept of organic evolution. E. B. Tyler of England and L. H. Morgan of the United States were foremost among these early theorists who saw anthropology mainly as a natural science concerned with prehistoric, contemporary non-literate and non-European peoples. Assembled data on these various peoples, though incomplete, led the compilers to attempt an assignment of all men to stages of "progress" from savagery through barbarism to civilization. The Australian aborigines were placed at one end of the line of development, the white Europeans at the other. Thus, unilinear evolutionists theorized that cultural growth could be understood as a single line of development from the simple to the complex; culture itself had its roots in a kind of psychic unity. This led to a belief that all men had the same potential for development but had been held back by such factors as climate, soil, lack of experience, and so on. The evolutionists believed they had proof that even civilized man had passed through these stages of development. This proof lay in the "survivals" which remained in modern man's behavior— belief in witches, ghosts and other superstitions. Such theories of unilinear progressive development of culture from a single point of origin are quite fictitious from an historical point of view. They cannot be verified when actual and sufficient data are tested.

The accumulation of data, professionally gathered as time passed by direct observations in the field, pointed up the discrepancies in the "stage" theory of progress. As the American frontier reached the Pacific, the changing climate of opinion gathered momentum. The doctrine of a universal scheme of unilinear evolution encountered a flood of data that discredited it completely in science, only to survive as a part of socialist and communist political dogma. Friedrich Engels fitted unilinear evolutionism to the socialist pattern, and Karl Marx gave the idea his blessing. The reasoning, condensed, runs thus: Culture has evolved everywhere through the same stages, although some peoples evolve faster than others. Morgan and the capitalist anthropologists did not see that capitalism is a transitional stage, and that socialism is the coming and final society. The evolutionists' thinking thus was incorporated and still persists in the Communistic dialectic.

More recently, there has been a modified revival of theory relating to total cultural development. The work of Robert Braidwood is fairly representative of the "neo-revolutionary" viewpoint. One cannot question whether cultural evolution has occurred. Men repeatedly search for evolutionary uniformities, which may be identified only by an enormous amount of historical research. Braidwood sees these uniformities best presented by types of economy. He thus classifies man's development according to his economic activities—food gathering, incipient agriculture and animal domestication, primary village farming efficiency, and incipient urbanization. The discovery of an adequate food supply, dependable the year round, was required before large concentrations of people in any one area were possible.

Although the method of the early evolutionists as well as their philosophy has been challenged and discredited, positive contributions of these theorists must not be lost sight of. The earlier concept of *culture* was brought into sharper focus in their thinking. They also saw that culture and race should not be confused when studying human behavior. Furthermore, they drew attention to sub-divisions of culture termed *aspects,* and made clear the value of studying the problems that fall within these subdivisions of cultural behavior.

Historicalism

The tendency of the cultural evolutionists to draw bits and pieces of behavior from all over the world out of time sequence, and place them into predetermined categories, obviously was scientifically unsound. Nevertheless, although dissatisfaction with theories thus formulated was mounting, the first serious challenge did not come until Franz Boas, an American anthropologist, by means of a method which was strictly empirical, proposed to study culture by investigating the relationships of specific behavioral elements within the total culture of the tribe or society practicing them. Important as well, he believed, was the geographical distribution of these behavioral elements among neighboring areas. Subsequent research into these aspects of culture led to the development of a distinctive terminology. For instance, a minimum significant unit of behavior capable of being isolated in time and space was termed a culture *trait*, while an inter-related trait group became known as a culture *complex*.

Analysis of the geographic distribution of culture traits made apparent the fact that similar traits could be identified over specific areas. Thus arose the term *culture area*, designating a group of societies with a greater or lesser degree of interaction, practicing more or less similar ways of living. Examination of the process of trait distribution contributed other new concepts which became part of the working vocabulary of the historicists. Independent invention and diffusion were suggested as possible reasons for the appearance of similar traits in different societies (as opposed to the psychic unity concept of the evolutionists). In turning their attention to culture contact between peoples, specific units of culture settings, both past and present, were considered. As their methodology was mainly comparative, the historicists were involved in considerable "field" work—actual participant observation. Here they achieved a high level of objectivity and accumulated carefully assembled field data, refuting the evolutionists' theories, as well as the thinking of racial, geographic, and economic determinists.

As with cultural evolutionism, the approach to the study of culture initiated by Boas developed inadequacies as it was expanded. Statistical handling of traits led such anthropologists as Clark Wissler to propose unsound culture area theories that cultural distribution occurred in a mechanical manner. He suggested, for instance, in his "Age Area" theory, that the passage of time would insure the spread of traits from one area to another—the older the trait, the more widespread its occurrence. Thus, Hinduism, the older belief system, should be more widespread than

Buddhism. This, of course, is not the case, since Hinduism is not a proselytizing religion. No consideration was given either to the individuals involved in the process or the nature of the trait itself. The concentration of interest on units of culture tended to draw attention away from the individual, who was treated as a passive unit upon which the active culture impressed itself.

On the positive side, however, historicism made clear the desirability of identifying the unit elements of culture and studying these specific behaviorial units within the context of the culture concerned. Their comparative method and objective field work gave a firm basis to generalizations about culture which for the first time were abstractions from observed behavior. Concepts introduced by the historicists compose an important part of the thinking and vocabulary of today's anthropologists.

Functionalism

Although Boas and the historicists had implied the connections between the "parts" and the "whole" of a culture, it remained for two anthropologists, at a later date, to make these connections explicit. B. Malinowski working among the Trobriand Islanders, and A. R. Radcliffe-Brown with the Andaman Islanders, both published monographs at about the same time, analyzing cultural behavior by means of a functional approach. This "school" arose as a physiological analogy; customs were compared to the muscles, bones, etc., of an organism and were regarded as parts of culture, which were to be considered as interacting parts of a sort of organic whole. Although Radcliffe-Brown recognized the analogy and treated it as such—useful pedagogically but not rigorously scientific—Malinowski apparently did not deal critically with it.

An example of the functional point of view can be seen in an examination of the Trobriand Kula exchanges. Malinowski describes these as an exchange of ceremonial goods between the peoples of a number of different communities. The exchanges were made roughly in a ring pattern. He understood these trading patterns to be surrounded by elaborate social and magical activities which were related to all phases of their lives. He concluded that it was necessary, therefore, to examine the total meaning and context of these exchanges in terms of not only each culture concerned, but also the intercultural relations involved. As a result of his research, Malinowski postulated that any behavioral unit was a response made to satisfy the individual's purposes or "needs." Thus, all men had basic drives and the "need" to satisfy these drives led to primary, derived and integrative responses which were culturally shaped. The behavior thus developed served the function of satisfying one or another kind of "need."

Radcliffe-Brown, on the other hand, focused his analysis on the contribution made by various elements to the maintenance of the social structure. In studying incest regulations, for instance, he felt that they had developed to prevent confusion or conflict between members of the society. They thus functioned as an integrating custom. Cross-cultural studies led him to believe that some societies were in greater equilibrium than others, i.e., they were healthier. He accordingly noted that some societies tended toward a healthy integration of all parts, while others tended toward dysfunction. The key ideas of both men, however, were focused on the system as having primary importance; that all units of behavior of the system are secondary and determined by the system.

Anthropologists who have organized their thinking on functional lines have been criticized for their failure to consider the part played by the individual in establishing behavioral relationships. They also paid little attention to the relation of society to culture, or to the processes of change. On the positive side, however, the functional system of thought was a new and vigorous approach to understanding cultural behavior. Concepts employed here have since undergone much further study in both anthropology and other behavioral sciences. Out of the functional view developed the configurational, "psychological" approach to the study of cultural integration.

Configurationalism

Since 1930, many anthropologists have treated cultures as relatively unique and integrated entities, and concentrated on symbolic or psychological aspects of the society. These were conceived

as shaping social and individual dimensions of behavior. Edward
Sapir and Ruth Benedict, both students of Franz Boas, spear-
headed this approach to the study of human behavior.

Sapir's early studies were mainly in the field of language. His
focus on language as a cultural experience led him to propose that
it was a major factor in directing the thoughts of the users—that
individuals speaking one pattern of symbols had potentials or limi-
tations on their thinking not known to users of other languages.
Later, he applied to culture as a whole many of the concepts
developed in his earlier work. He proposed that all human
behavior is symbolic; and that its meanings are shared and communicated to group members. Sapir generalized that the true
objective entities were abstracted configurations of idea and action
patterns with endlessly different meanings for the various individuals whose different experiences in the group formed the meanings.
His interest in the vital relation between culture and the individual
set the stage for a new direction of inquiry.

Following up Sapir's work, Ruth Benedict undertook studies
among the Pueblo peoples whom she noted were quite different
from neighboring tribes. Borrowing from Nietzsche, she described
the Pueblo cultures as "Apollonian," emphasizing external or
extrovertive forms of behavior: ritualistic, conformist, avoiding
excesses, and so on. Neighboring tribes were, she felt, "Dionysian"
or introvertive: individualistic, aggressive, valuing violent experience, self-motivated rather than group oriented. Thus, she applied
"psychological" terms, which formerly had been applied only to
describe individuals, to describe the configuration of all peoples
within the culture.

She concluded that each culture develops a fairly consistent
pattern of thought and action, with characteristic purposes and
emotional and intellectual configuration which permeate the whole
culture. This configuration orients members of the culture to
more or less consistent behavior and responses. Morris Opler of
Cornell University pointed out that in a complex society there
would be more than one such dominant configuration and proposed
the concept of "themes" as an alternative way of expressing this
intrinsic aspect of culture.

An extension of Benedict's initial analysis led to a series of
studies aimed at understanding the "normal" personality in any

group. Later inquiry was also directed toward the manner in which new members of the society were guided or shaped into the kind of persons "desired" by the adult members. As a great portion of "character" development was thought to be unconscious patterning, a distinction arose between direct and indirect learning processes as well as between explicit and implicit preparation for membership in any specific culture.

Change Theory

The last word in theory—observed relationships between various phenomena—is, of course, not yet set forth. As man understands more about human behavior, new insights emerge. The trend in theory ranged from the early theorists' concentration on large scale wholes and cultural change, to more recent emphasis on specific units. In the latter instance, behavior is examined at a single time level. Even more recently, though by no means well organized as yet, has developed an interest in studying factors which change behavior or hold it consistent. Theorists interested in this aspect of cultural behavior look to innovation, invention and cultural contact to understand behavioral change. It is suggested that continuities in behavior result from training given, directly or indirectly, implicitly or explicitly, by the society to each oncoming generation.

Theorists generally take the stand that the individual and only the individual can initiate change. Such an individual, generally referred to as the *donor,* in current literature, is believed to be supported or reinforced in his efforts to bring about change by others interacting within the same or related activities. The donor is given the "right" by the society to present certain kinds of behavior. For instance, the teacher is sanctioned for the presentation of specific cultural behavior, but normally he would not be allowed to write medical prescriptions. The status thus filled by the donor involves not only rights but also obligations to others and expectations of others' relationships to himself.

A number of variables, identified in the process of acceptance of change, cannot be completely set forth in this particular article. Among the foremost variables, however, is the prestige of the donor as well as of the *cluster* which reinforces him; continued and concentrated contact with the source of innovation and the nature of the new behavior are also considered of importance. In other words, the "fit" of the innovative behavior in the general cultural milieu depends on readiness to accept change. Change theorists have also found it useful to distinguish between the content and form of behavior. Other factors being equal, forms are more easily transmitted than are complete cultural meanings.

This monograph is mainly concerned with the process of enculturation—the total culture presented to individuals within the society which shapes both their ideas and action patterns. At the same time, it considers the aspect of cultural change and the problem of incorporating into the educational system new ideas and action patterns emerging in our rapidly changing milieu. It is essential to our cultural way of life that these new patterns become cultural—capable of being shared and learned by those members of the society who must assimilate them. Furthermore, although examining the patterned, modal behavior, the starting point is always considered to be the individual. The individual is considered to be a complex "person . . . representing an interplay not only of genetic, habitat, cultural and social determinants, but also personal variation in perception and decision."[1]

---

[1] Felix Keesing, *Cultural Anthropology* (New York: Holt, Rinehart and Winston, Inc., 1962).

Chapter 3

Major Divisions of Anthropology

The science of anthropology is divided into two broad fields: *physical* and *cultural*. Physical anthropologists are interested in problems of human biology: human evolution or biological processes in contemporary human groups. Cultural anthropology has produced scholars who specialize in one of three areas: prehistoric archaeology, linguistics, or social anthropology. Archaeologists investigate and analyze those aspects of man's cultural development that shed light on his early life during the period of about a million years before the invention of writing. The linguist is concerned with varied patterns of speech and thought that have developed in the long ages of man's use of his peculiarly human ability to talk.

The integrating factor in this diversity of subject matter lies in the anthropologist's consideration conjointly of all phases of man's life, biological and cultural, past and present. A combination of these varied subjects gives anthropologists the broadest, least segmented, most free-ranging approach to understanding human behavior. It is thus of special and profound importance to today's educator.

Physical Anthropology

Physical anthropology studies man, the animal: such factors as the nature of racial differences, inheritance of bodily traits, the growth and maturation of the human organism, and the relationship between man and his natural habitat. Briefly stated, the physical anthropologist studies human variation and human adaptation. He is also interested in the way man's unique attribute —culture—affects and is affected by biological factors.

He searches for remains of early man and compares them with modern man. Although there are still many gaps in the historical sequences which the physical anthropologist builds, he knows what early man looked like, when he first appeared, and how his bodily characteristics have changed during his time on earth. He can indicate the areas where man first lived. Through related sciences such as paleontology, embryology, and geology, the physical anthropologist traces the evolution of man from his non-human ancestors through the physical changes which gradually produced, about 35,000 years ago, the form of man, homo sapiens, which we know today.

The development of upright posture freed man's hands to use tools, making possible a better adaptation to his habitat. The growth of his cerebrum, especially the memory cells, made possible the storing of knowledge which he could transmit to the next generation. One age, thus, stood on the shoulders of each and every preceding age. The development of human vocal organs with their great range of sound possibilities, together with man's ability to symbolize and his other physical changes set man off from other animals and made him unique in the animal kingdom.

Existing physical types, whether classified as Caucasoid, Negroid, or Mongoloid, are to be regarded as composing a single species. Anthropologists generally think that the so-called "races" did not develop until fairly recent times, approximately 35,000 years ago. Race, in all probability, is the result of the constant adjustment of biological organisms to varied geographical settings. Howells suggests that many of the observable characteristics of man are the result of natural selection, the survival and propagation of those types best adapted to their habitat. For example, the dark skin of the Negro is an adaptation to the force of sunlight, while the Mongoloid eyes, set in protective fat-lined lids, flat forehead and broad cheek are ideal for protection against the bitterly cold weather which came with the last glacial period.

However, the observed differences in individuals of various races do not justify a subdivision of the species. Continual inter-breeding of the so-called races through the years has virtually eliminated the possibility of the existence of a "pure race." Populations vary one from another in the relative frequency of genes occurring in each. Race differences consist of variations in bodily structure which are determined primarily by the genes.

It can be generally stated that greater differences appear in the bodily features of individuals within any human race than in the averages of such features as these are used to characterize races. Races should be recognized for what they are—categories based on outer appearance that permit us to make convenient classifications of human materials. To understand this fact is an important initial step in assessing the biological nature of man and the relation of this aspect to his culture building abilities. Man's traditions and culture are transmitted socially, not biologically. Man's cultural behavior and his biological inheritance—race—vary independently. In other words, there is no significant correlation between the distribution of genetic characteristics and the distribution of culture.

Data furnished by the physical anthropologist thus take on importance to the educator. Accurate comparisons of racial groups are not possible unless adequate criteria for classification and universally valid methods of measurement are forthcoming. Although criteria are currently in existence, universal application would be impossible in practice. No one, therefore, may say that races are unequal, nor can one say they are equal. The white man has constructed intelligence tests that demonstrate his racial superiority. The Chinese have shown with similar tests and equal finality the superlative qualities of their own groups. Obviously, therefore, tests may be devised in which persons reared in one society will attain high scores; those reared among other people will score low. No culture-free intelligence tests exist. Nor has it been shown that scores achieved result from racial, hereditary differences. Thus, no conclusive results may be expected from mental tests which attempt to demonstrate racial superiority of one race over another. Any normal child, regardless of race, can be trained to any other culture if put from the start into the appropriate learning situation.

The physical anthropologist makes quite clear that popular notions of race are prejudiced and inaccurately framed in terms of bodily details accidentally emphasized. Too often, too little consideration, if any, is given to the social and cultural restrictions which deny to individuals of certain races full participation in the activities of the society.

As far as psychological capacities are concerned, the anthropologist has observed that individuals respond with differing efficiency to ordinary experiences. One person may respond more readily to musical sounds while another is alerted only to visual beauty, and still another, to abstractions. It is quite conceivable that such specialized behavioral tendencies are in part due to genetic potentialities. The anthropologist does assume, however, that so far as these "psychological" reactions of the individual have genetic basis, the same world-wide process of differentiation and distribution would have been at work as in the evolution of bodily characteristics.

Granted that psychological preferences and sensitivities may in part stem from biological factors, even superficial observation will reveal their direct relation to cultural examples, pressures, and expectations. An individual could be born with the best apparatus in the world for becoming a great singer, but if his society devalued singing, it is more than likely that he would never realize his potential. By the same token, a man inherently aggressive, born into a gentle, uncompetitive society might well grow up without conspicuous expression of such alleged inheritance. Thus, the physical anthropologist makes apparent that man's unique attribute—culture—affects and is affected by biological factors.

Cultural Anthropology

Prehistoric Archaeology

The archaeologist investigates the evidences from cultures of peoples long since vanished and long buried. By means of various techniques which utilize other sciences—physics, chemistry, geology, anatomy, and others—the archaeologist reconstructs a picture of former ways of life; their artifacts are his paints. Basic methods of excavation take the geological setting fully into account, stratification is carefully recorded, and finds are classified in relation to their relative position. Often the archaeologist works with tweezers and a toothbrush. The totality of his work allows him also to infer something about the nonmaterial aspects of man's life in earlier periods.

The archaeologist also traces the origins and historical development of man's past activities. Much of what we know of more recent human culture is based on written records that have been preserved. Relatively speaking, however, writing is a very new invention in the history of man. Human cultures began developing more than a million years ago; writing appeared only about three thousand years before the Christian era. The prehistoric archaeologist, concerned with cultures that antedate written records, must rely only on material remains.

Our debt to prehistoric man is an impressive one. Practically all the discoveries of basic techniques that mark the present day— except metal working, power driven machinery, and electricity— were made during the period of time with which the archaeologist deals. Early man's particular contribution to the educator is in the long view of human activity, especially in those aspects of culture on which his excavated data are most eloquent: technology, settlement patterns and art styles. He also gives us observable proof of man's ability to adapt to a changing physical, social, and cultural world.

Comparative Linguistics

The province of the anthropological linguist encompasses all languages, ancient and modern, those of literate and non-literate peoples. He is interested in the origin, development, and structure of languages, just as he is concerned with the relationship of languages to man's other learned behavior.

In all probability, human speech evolved from animal cries. However, it is not known when or how man took the steps to symbolize ideas by grouping sounds. A study of sub-human or early human fossils for clues tells us nothing of the beginning of speech, for the section of the brain which controls speech in men is also present in the other anthropoids. A search among animals of different species also is fruitless. Though animals can be taught to react to signs—to see an association between words or acts and things—they cannot be taught to talk.

Analysis of the languages of the extant "primitive" peoples also fails to clear up the questions of origins. All mankind can speak. Although their languages are constructed quite differently, there is no indication that any language is more "primitive" than any other. All are equally capable—though none wholly so—of expressing the thoughts deemed necessary of expression. As societies develop new ideas or artifacts, new vocabulary is added. Thus, any language is capable of saying what needs to be said.

The anthropological linguist studies the structure of languages by highly technical analyses of forms of speech, phonetic patterns and the consistency of their use, dialectic variation, and so forth. He reconstructs the history of languages and language groups. Thus, he compares one language with another to determine what, if any, features are common to all languages. By these two means —the reconstruction and comparison of languages and language groups—he seeks to understand the processes by which languages came into being and acquired their present-day diversity.

Of great importance to the educator is this fact: language makes culture possible, and culture is the phenomenon from which education springs and is maintained. Language, as a purely human and non-instinctive method of communicating ideas, emotions and desires, must be learned. Linguistic communication is accomplished by means of arbitrarily assigned symbols. Language has come into existence only when individuals have experienced some event in common, attached a common value to it, assigned an arbitrarily chosen sound combination to its expression, and communicated it by repeating such sounds. Non-spoken symbols, as gestures, and ultimately, written symbols, are developed in the same way. In other words, we express experience in language. Through language we communicate with others. By the language used, the individual indicates, among other things, his status or social position, his education, and his home region. His choice of words also tells his listener whether he is communicating ideas from everyday living, formal occasions, or special ceremonial or religious rites. Thus, language is not only the storehouse of human experience and the tool by which this experience is transmitted from generation to generation, but also it tells about the cultural background of its users.

The anthropological linguist contributes one further insight to the educator. A person learning one language tends to perceive and conceive of the world in a different fashion from people who have learned another. As languages differ, and as the symbolic representation of words is the result of events or experiences held in common, it follows that users of diverse languages perceive seemingly similar events differently. This applies not only to things and actions but also to basic ideas of time, space, and causation. Edward Sapir suggests that man can neither think nor reason without a language. If this is so, then language shapes even the thinking process. Sapir inferred that thought can grow only as language grows, and that an idea cannot "attain to individual and independent life until it has found a distinctive linguistic embodiment."[2]

Applied close to home, it is evident that peoples of different classes or sub-cultures develop symbolic communication built on experiences peculiar to their status. Thus, Americans who differ culturally according to region or social background may "see" our society differently—perhaps with regard to vital values—and cannot, by the very nature of their vocabulary, "think" about it in the same way. Even closer to home, education must transmit either directly through language, or indirectly in other ways the essential experiences on which our cultural values rest, if this or any society based on these values is to continue.

Cultural Foundations of Education

Man has been called the human animal. Like other animals, man inherits his capacity to learn as well as certain biological drives which may predispose him to various activities. An overwhelming preponderance of his behavior, however, can be accounted for only in terms of socially acquired, culturally determined and transmitted patterns of action and thinking. His in-

---

[2] Edward Sapir, *Language* (New York: Harcourt, Brace & World, Inc., 1921), p. 17. For other reading in this general area, see reference bibliography IV, Linguistics.

herent animal "instincts" are constantly controlled and shaped by acquired habit systems. These acquired modes of behavior are the direct result of interstimulation with other human beings. The specific patterning of interstimulation and the kinds of behavior allowed in any given society are all part of his cultural heritage. It can become part of each individual's behavior only if it is presented to him, and if he in turn learns it. Thus, education may be considered to be the means by which the animal—man—becomes the human being. Each culture structures its educational system to teach behavior which the group finds desirable. It is obvious, of course, that conflict arises in a heterogeneous society as different groups define "desirable" differently. Nonetheless, in this fashion each individual is molded into a person representative of his group and his society.

If any cultural mode of life is continued, each society must establish some means for the transmission of its customs, beliefs, and knowledge, i.e., education. By education, the anthropologist means more than schooling. In our society, the schools undertake a great deal of the responsibility for transmitting our cultural accumulation. There are many peoples, however, who do not have or need schools. In these societies, behavioral necessities are taught by kin members or peers in the context of everyday living. Nor are schools the only system of indoctrination in our society. Both child and adult are continually exposed to influences outside the formal school structure. Families, peers, mass media, playmates, and often total strangers constantly present various forms of cultural behavior. Children, who once reached the classroom with a relatively similar background, today face first grade filled with visual and auditory impressions gleaned from the family's favorite television channel.

This total accumulation of learned behavior makes us twentieth-century Americans. Sub-cultural learning makes different kinds of Americans. Similarly, various behavioral patterns preferred and taught by other peoples stamp their members as belonging to their culture. This can be accomplished in only one way, either directly or indirectly, through the educational process—the total process by which the individual, child or adult, acquires the knowledge, understanding attitudes, and orientations that are characteristic of this culture.

Chapter 4

What Is Presented?

An answer to this question involves seven basic concepts, namely, culture, diffusion, cultural prescriptives, cultural alternatives, cultural patterns, content, and values.

Culture[3]

People live together in societies, which differ according to what individuals born in a society usually learn. Habits acquired by an American differ in almost every detail from those learned by an Australian aboriginie—and these in turn differ from those acquired by a Vietnamese. Whatever the tribe or nation, one can live among his fellows only by acquiring the habits approved and practiced locally. These forms of learned behavior followed in a society are spoken of as cultural behavior. Culture, accordingly,

---

[3] Douglas G. Haring, *Personal Character and Cultural Milieu* (Syracuse, New York: Syracuse University Press, 1956), *passim.*

denotes an abstracted totality of learned and socially transmitted behavior.

Forms of behavior observed in social activities among any people may be described; such descriptions of customs, habits, and values—i.e., assumptions that shape the actions and decisions of the participants—have provided anthropologists with a wealth of important facts of cultural behavior. Patterns of behavior learned and followed by various peoples are everywhere *unique,* yet are often roughly comparable with practices observed elsewhere. No culture presents esoteric mysteries beyond the power of outsiders to comprehend, for what one human being can learn another can learn, given patience and the will to understand. The process of learning *how* to live in any environment (including geographical habitat and social and cultural milieu) has evolved in an historically influenced relationship between man and nature, man and his ideas of natural and supernatural, and man and other men; all modes of living are composed of learned responses to a locally current milieu of stimulating situations. These complex repertories of learned responses are not everywhere the same, for there are virtually limitless possible combinations of behavioral elements. In every area people exhibit the unique cultural responses they have learned in the context of a specific background.

Culture is *accumulative.* New forms of cultural behavior are being devised constantly; the patterns of behavior that may be learned have been increasing in number throughout human history—slowly in the millennia of prehistory, more rapidly as each new accomplishment, extended the range of the humanly possible, and explosively with the rise of mechanical technologies. For over a million years men have been learning and inventing. While some old cultural patterns disappear as more effective replacements are invented, certain basic patterns of interaction have continued despite changes in outward forms. However imposing these changes in forms, such cultural systems as family, economic behavior, political organization, and education continue wherever human beings live together. Cultural forms disappear as more effective replacements are invented, although memories of the outmoded forms may persist, and many of them could be revived if circumstances required. The ancient Egyptian practice of mummifying their prestigious dead, for example, disappeared when their kingdom collapsed, even as the horse and buggy have become curiosities since the advent of the motor car. Thus cultural accumulation continues to expand at an accelerating rate.

Forms of cultural behavior may be and usually are *diffused*— not only from person to person but from one tribe or nation to another. As peoples come into contact, ideas, games, technologies, folklore, organizational patterns, religious philosophies—all the kaleidoscopic details of ways of living are copied or exchanged. Whether the exchange is subtle and unnoticed or tumultuous, whatever its content, these complex processes are summarized in the term *cultural diffusion*. The late Ralph Linton humorously reminds his readers in *The Study of Man* (1936) of the role of diffusion in the building of their own culture:

> "Our solid American citizen awakens in a bed built on a pattern which originated in the Near East but which was modified in Northern Europe before it was transmitted to America. He throws back covers made from cotton, domesticated in India, or linen, domesticated in the Near East, or wool from sheep, also domesticated in the Near East, or silk, the use of which was discovered in China . . . He slips into his moccasins, invented by the Indians of the Eastern woodlands . . . takes off his pajamas, a garment invented in India, and washes with soap invented by the ancient Gauls . . . begins breakfast with an orange, from the eastern Mediterranean, a canteloupe from Persia or perhaps a piece of African Watermelon . . . He reads the news of the day imprinted in characters invented by the ancient Semites upon a material invented in China by a process invented in Germany. As he absorbs the accounts of foreign troubles he will, if he is a good conservative citizen, thank a Hebrew deity in an Indo-European language that he is a 100 per cent American."[4]

No current situation is entirely understandable without taking into account the cultural backgrounds of its interstimulating members. An American teacher cannot with full assurance interpret responses of her students to specific stimuli unless she knows the cultural background of each. New trends toward district and integrated school systems compound the problem. A heterogeneous classroom group may be as difficult to comprehend

---

[4] Ralph Linton, *The Study of Man* (New York: Appleton-Century, 1936), pp. 326-27.

and lead as a gathering of the United Nations; different cultural backgrounds involve different ways of perceiving and conceiving the classroom situation.

Cultural Prescriptives

Linton conceived of culture as composed of identifiable elements that could be classified in categories. The ideas, habits, and conditioned responses common to all "sane" adult members of a society he termed *universals*. Thus used, the term applied only to cultural elements in a particular society. As this term is consistently used elsewhere to designate worldwide similarities, i.e., family systems, religious behavior, political behavior, and so on, confusion arises even though by definition Linton gives it a narrower meaning. To avoid such confusion, the term *prescriptive* is used to express current behavior that each individual must learn and practice to achieve minimum adaptation in his cultural milieu: the use of the "native" language, patterns of housing and clothing, the three "R's" (in our society), patterns of etiquette, values, goals, and so on. Although all societies transmit behavior that falls into this category, specific societies include different elements. For instance, the prescriptive language, varies throughout the world, yet everywhere language exists; anti-incest prescriptives also are universal, yet specific restrictions vary.

Cultural Alternatives

Every culture has traits shared by certain individuals, but not by all members of the society. These elements are termed *alternatives*. Although Linton used this concept to represent different reactions to the same situation or different techniques for achieving the same ends, it is used here less specifically. Alternative behavior represents elements not classed as prescriptive, i.e., any elements not deemed essential learning for all sane, adult members for minimum adaptation. In our society all must be "educated"—individuals must learn arithmetic, English, writing, and so on. These are some of our prescriptives. All individuals need not acquire domestic skills, calculus, and the latest dance steps, i.e., the alternatives.

Cultural Patterns

Normative elements of any culture take on designs representing individual behavior patterns practiced by members of the society. These patterns give coherence, continuity, and distinctive form to the way of life of the people manifesting them. Cultural patterning has two complimentary aspects: explicit behavior characteristically taken, and psychological values implicitly understood. These implicit values influence the explicit forms practiced. Different values are evidenced in different forms. This may be seen, for example, in the mating patterns of Americans and certain Melanesians. Choice of mate is exercised by individuals in one, dictated by families in the other. There is a wide range of ages at which marriage may be contracted in America, while in Melanesia marriage age is relatively fixed. In our society, the transfer of valuable goods during bethrothal and at the time of marriage is secondary and informal; in Melanesia both are essential and highly regularized. Yet in each, the "proper" way is explicitly and implicitly recognized. Furthermore, members of each society can describe the "proper" patterns if questioned.[5]

Very early in life, different patterns of behavior are presented to prepare individuals for different interests, goals and expectations. Patterning is influenced by class and caste systems, occupational differentiation, age, sex, subcultural traditions, ethnic groups, and so on. Thus, the term cultural pattern includes overt acts and covert values that provide motivation for action. The pattern phenomenon in culture is "the reflection of the common elements in the individual behavior of those who live in the culture into which they have been born."[6]

Values

Values are affectively (emotionally) charged tendencies to action which involve preferences and often conscious choices among alternatives. Explicit and implicit value orientations make

---

[5] Melville Herskovits, *Cultural Anthropology* (New York: Alfred A. Knopf, Inc., 1955), pp. 410-29.
[6] *Ibid.*

up the value system within a cultural system. All societies live
by certain expressed or non-expressed "rules" of behavior—vital
attitudes which lie largely below the level of individual conscious-
ness but which at all times influence one's behavior. Such
evaluative attitudes involve habitual certainty that some behavior
is "right," "good," and "just," while other behavior may be
deemed "wrong," "bad," or "unjust." These value judgements
provide powerful central motivation to certain kinds of behavior.
The concept of equality, for instance, leads thousands of Americans to strive for racial integration, while the idea of racism
inspires behavior directed against integration.

Values such as these, held deeply by members of a society, function as consolidating or disrupting agents. Many non-literate,
sacred societies are integrated around a single dominant value.
On the other hand, American society manifests conflicting values
and lacks the cohesiveness characteristic of tribal or peasant
societies.

Emotionally charged values tend to impede cultural change.
Instigators of change must initiate changes in attitudes (value
reorientation)—at least for a large number of individuals in any
society—by force or persuasion before new behavior is accepted
and institutionalized.

By studying many cultures, each on its own terms, anthropologists have discovered that each society has its own value system,
its own standards and evaluations of behavior. There is a difference
between objective scientific description of a society and its culture,
and the individual observer's acceptance of values in his own
conduct. Values held by others may be observed and described
without accepting them for one's own behavior—except as one
may honestly accept certain values observed in an alien society
as better than those he has personally held. But scientific study
in itself is purely descriptive, and values held in different societies
are perceived in their context as purely relative to that context.
The scientist does not judge the values held by others; this is the
task of philosophy, and all of us are philosophers when it comes to
decisions affecting personal conduct. Every value system is relative
to the cultural context in which it is discovered. For any society,
the "right" and "wrong" habits of individuals embody and maintain
the value system of their culture. Female infanticide, for example,
is considered wrong and criminal by Americans; such a practice,

however, may be approved or prescriptive in a tribe that puts some of the girl babies to death to hold population within the limits of the available food. Such drastic measures may be considered "right" where the practice is the only known way of controlling population in a region of limited sustenance, as in Tibet or in certain islands of Polynesia.

This relativity of values does not support ruthless extermination of minorities as a political measure in large "modern" nations in which contrary values are historically and currently accepted. The Nazi extermination of Jews occurred in a nation where millions of people held to a more humanitarian moral code but were unable or unwilling to protest. Cultural relativity is no excuse for "barbarity" imposed by tyrants in violation of the value system of a "civilized" society; cultural relativity is a scientific concept necessary to the understanding of diverse societies, and implies no personal acceptance of the values an anthropologist discovers in his study.

Content

"Culture and Personality" specialists distinguish three features in the learning situation: content, context, and emotional quality associated with learning. The *content* of learning is the substance of *what* is presented or acquired. The polite "Please sit down," the mechanics of making a cake or a kite, the system of calculus, the concept of equality, all represent instances of content, i.e., skills, manners, postures, feelings, sentiments, and ideals that are presented to people for assimilation in the course of their lifetime.

The *context* of learning refers to the social and biological circumstances accompanying presentation of content—the age and sex of the individual, his level of learning, and his state of preparedness for the present content. It also includes the way in which content is presented—directly or indirectly, in a formal or informal setting.

Some degree of *emotional response* pervades every learning situation. Such affective relationships, whether consciously or unconsciously assimilated by the learner, remain with him as part of the total learning, and affect later responses that may involve aspects of the original stimuli.

What Is Presented?

There is not the slightest evidence that social behavior can be transmitted biologically from parent to child. Since human beings never behave socially in ways they have not learned, every society must establish some method of presenting its cultural base to each oncoming generation. Behavioral elements are presented, in a broad sense, as prescriptives or alternatives. Prescriptives vary inter-culturally and intra-culturally. Our culture, for instance, stresses the importance of competition in a myriad of situations; children are taught to be competitive. This is not the case among the Samoans, to cite a single example; there, competitiveness and precociousness are considered undesirable and are discouraged by adults. Or again, a generation ago in our society all were taught to glorify work for work's sake; today this belief often lacks conviction, if it is presented at all.

Although every society must insure continuance of custom by presenting its traditions to the oncoming generation, no civilized individual ever encounters the total cultural repertoire. Early man, in a far less complex situation, divided activities. He presented some behavior to women only, other to men. Such divisions were based mainly on age and sex. By far the greatest part of the culture was presented to all. Any individual, in an emergency, could perform all essential activities. Specialization was kept at a minimum, and at least a few individuals learned all there was to know.

However, increasing division of labor and population result in diminished awareness of the total picture for all. Individuals may be vaguely aware of a larger range of cultural behavior than has been presented purposefully to them, but awareness of behavior and ability to perform it are quite different. Modern man, in an emergency, may be quite helpless in meeting essential requirements of existence.

Elements that compose the major portion of the cultural base of most pre-literate societies may, therefore, be classified as prescriptives. In our society, when considering the total cultural base, by far the greatest part of each individual's behavior falls in the category of alternatives. Pre-literate societies present the prescriptive ideas, habits, and conditioned responses in the context of everyday living within the family group. As children reach varying levels of maturation, different kinsfolk may be involved in the enculturation process.

In our society, however, major prescriptives are presented outside of the family unit. The school system presents a high percentage of the prescriptives that are sanctioned by dominant group members, institutionalized and transmitted as part of the cultural tradition. This deeply rooted system resists change even when change is imperative. Outside the formal school system, family, church, and peer group members may present prescriptives in conflict with those presented by the school. In other words, there is considerable conflict on the part of major presenting agencies as to what behavior is essential—what prescriptives should be presented and reinforced.

In the folklore of the time, one commonly hears one set of prescriptives from peers, another from a different generation: "Never tell the whole truth to your parents about your behavior; it upsets them too much." "Don't cheat with the teacher in the room." "Don't tell on a friend." "When pinned, don't date anyone else." "Go along with the group." Among peers of teen age, such are allegedly valuable lessons for "survival." Parents, on the other hand, offer different lessons: "Don't talk to strangers." "Work hard for success." "Now, when I was your age . . ." "Stand on your own two feet." "Nice girls don't . . ." Teachers also tend to be traditionally oriented, presenting prescriptives that the teenager finds difficult to put into practice: "Honesty is the best policy." "If you cheat, you cheat yourself." "Be an individual." "You must work hard to get along."

Elements chosen for prescriptive presentation should be consistent throughout the society if it is to be well integrated. This is accomplished in traditionally oriented societies. Our own problem is compounded by acceleration of cultural change. Continual re-examination of prescriptives is essential to insure adequate adaptation of individuals to their physical and cultural surroundings. Elements should be shifted to alternative presentation as the changing milieu necessitates. For example, early man placed great emphasis on presenting behavioral patterns that aided the young in their relationship with physical surroundings. Inadequate tools or technology made such adaptation a major concern. Modern man has a different problem. Advanced technologies relieve him of much of his concern about nature. However, population expansion (more interacting people), and greater specialization (needed integration of activities) raise great difficulties. Man today is faced with constant frustrations in his relationships with other men. Yet this area of interaction and integration—the techniques of satisfactory interpersonal relationships—we delegate largely to alternative presentation.

Cultural alternatives are a function of plural societies, division of labor and specialization. Our immigration policy contributed to the development of many sub-cultural ethnic groups, each with its own "imported" cultural patterns. Many of these behavioral alternatives remain as part of their descendants' cultural heritage. Division of labor and specialization produce social inequalities. Individuals who occupy various stratified positions tend to transmit their specialties to their "own kind." Even in the United States this practice is increasingly prevalent.

Both biological and social factors influence *what* is presented. Biologically, innate ability, age and sex influence what is presented. An individual's ability and the level of his maturation are taken into consideration in the majority of instances. We are familiar with periods in a child's life when we feel he is ready for presentation of certain kinds of information or behavior. At nine months, he sits up; at eighteen months he walks; somewhere along the line, we teach him to talk.

Socially, such factors as "race," religious affiliation, and educational background (among others) limit full active participation in the society. Labor unions may function to prevent presentation of their behavior specialties to certain racial and ethnic groups. Secrets of the Ku Klux Klan are presented only to certain kinds of people. Guidance counselors, on the basis of "intelligence" tests direct students to some channels of learning while closing others. Class status plays a part in determining the alternatives that are presented to oncoming generations. "Upper class" children are taught behavior not presented to "lower class" children. In some world areas, certain occupations are virtually the property of caste members and their progeny.

Hereditary kinship prohibits transmission of related knowledge to all kin members. The Australian aboriginies exclude women from certain religious ceremonies. Men seldom learn (at least in our society) the secrets of the beauty parlor, while women know little about Masonic meetings. Thus, all peoples fail to present certain kinds of behavior to specified members of their respective societies. In other words, biological factors are not usually the basis of selectivity. Culturally determined assumptions prohibit presentation to all, and specify *who* has the *right* to learn such behavior. Individuals who learn a particular alternate behavior are also taught under what circumstances others may learn it.

Although all knowledge is transmitted culturally, individual selectivity alters what is presented in each new situation. Such selectivity is both intentional and unintentional. In Indonesia, for instance, individuals presenting Islam selected different elements, selected from beliefs of different "schools." After this intentional selectivity, teachers who adhered to these "schools" further altered the selected elements prior to presentation on the basis of their understanding. The cultural background of each affected this understanding—an unintentional selectivity. The result was an "Indonesian Islam" mystically oriented and allowing, among other things, worship of saints. It also absorbed earlier animistic, Hindu and Buddhist beliefs. Further unintentional modification resulted from linguistic misconceptions. As often as possible, Moslem teachers presented the teachings of Mohammed in the Holy language—Arabic. The few texts were written in Arabic. Difficult words in the body of the material were explained in the margins by more difficult words, in Arabic. Thus, at least in the earlier period of the Islamization of Indonesia, was presented an Islam highly colored by individual selectivity and modification.

This problem of selectivity and modification is not peculiar to inter-cultural situations. The work of Sapir and other linguists has alerted us to similar possibilities in intra-cultural communication. Vocabulary, for instance, is believed to be causally related to environment; words reflect the background of the user. People also perceive meaning in terms of their particular experiences.

This fact is made clear in a study by Bruner and Goodman, who found that children tend to overestimate the size of coins. In general, the amount of overestimation varies directly with the value of the coin. The error is greater with coins than with cardboard discs of the same size, and with poor children than with children of the well-to-do.[7] Thus, in a heterogeneous class, sub-cultural per-

---

[7] Theodore Brameld, *Cultural Foundations of Education* (New York: Harper & Row, Publishers 1957), p. 77.

ceptions of "meanings" of symbols may raise as real a problem in transmission of cultural behavior as do different languages.

In our society, it is true also that sub-cultural bias may unintentionally influence what an individual chooses to present. Brameld observes, for instance, that teachers (in the main from both sub-levels of the "middle class") ". . . tend not only to bias their teaching in the direction of their own status or those above them, but to reveal a bias against lower-class values. Since by far the largest group of students comes from the three lowest levels, the result is a great deal of conflict and waste in learning."[8]

It is not uncommon in the academic world to find students in a turmoil from apparent contradictions presented to them. Teachers trained in different disciplines offer conflicting explanations of cultural phenomenon. Geographic determinists neglect aspects that do not reinforce their point of view. In many states, teachers may not present facts about communism; the teaching of organic evolution is still outlawed in some areas.

In addition to selectivity based on discipline orientation, expectations of readiness also determine what is presented. Those responsible for presentation hold back content that they assume others are not "ready for." This phenomenon is common enough to politically minded individuals; colonial powers consistently denied freedom to underdeveloped countries for this reason. Margaret Mead found that various cultures look for readiness for a given piece of learning at different times. A particular item of learning may be so important to the society that a child may be hurried into it. In other instances, participation may await individual readiness or be delayed long after biological readiness. Any parent knows that a first child is hurried into talking and walking, while later children may be more casually raised. We also tend to hold back adulthood long after biological readiness.

Kluckhohn has raised an interesting question concerning the feasibility of teaching " . . . the child the ultimately correct type of behavior from the very outset, or when this is patently impossible, allow him to learn nothing until he becomes capable of learning precisely what will be ultimately expected of him as an

---

[8] *Ibid.*

adult member of society."[9] He adds that although " . . . no one has seriously advocated this sort of short-circuiting of the educational process in the technical sphere . . . in the realm of regulatory education, serious attempts have been made to make children conform from the very outset of their lives."[10]

Values—underlying, implicit beliefs—direct all transmission of cultural behavior, and shape the individual's response. Some values are presented as prescriptive, others as alternatives. Groups or classes of people have values unique to their way of life, while sharing to a greater or lesser degree prescriptive values. Benedict conceived of each culture as having its own characteristic "purposes," emotional and intellectual mainsprings," "configurations," and "goals" which pervaded behavior in the society concerned.[11] This is also true of sub-cultural groups. Shared meanings may integrate either the group or the total society, and such a value system gives a common cause to people who differ in so much of their other behavior.

Today these values are shifting. Traditional American culture was integrated around Puritan morality, the work-success ethic, achievement orientation, individualism, and so on. These values were presented as prescriptives to oncoming generations and incoming "foreigners." Such integrating beliefs are being replaced by an emerging character type that is outward oriented (conformity to the group). It is suggested that the social character of most individuals is split; different responses are called for in different situations with respect to different symbols. As noted, sub-groups tend to present different symbols with meanings unique to themselves. Thus, in a heterogeneous group, values and symbols believed to be held by all are, in fact, not so held. In other words, purposes, emotional and intellectual mainsprings, and goals are being presented as alternatives within sub-cultural groups, rather than as prescriptives to all members of our society.

Thus, the educational process has as its function the presentation

---

[9] Margaret Mead, *Continuities of Cultural Evolution* (New Haven: Yale University Press, 1965), p. 63.

[10] Clyde Kluckhohn, "The Educational Process," in *Exploring the Ways of Mankind,* Walter Goldschmidt (New York: Holt, Rinehart and Winston, Inc., 1960), p. 183.

[11] Ruth Benedict, *Patterns of Culture* (Boston: Houghton-Mifflin Co., 1934).

of cultural behavior both inter-generationally and intra-generationally. A major problem arises in knowing what to present to all, and what to present to selected individuals; perhaps, most important, what criteria will determine who is allowed to learn? Explicit and implicit prescriptives vital to a particular people at a particular time may lose their importance at another time under different circumstances. An educational system, responsible for transmission of prescriptive behavior, needs to be sensitive to shifting requirements of the total society. In an accelerating situation, with institutionalized and standardized school systems, this is perhaps impossible. Certain questions, however, must be raised. What important values today will be important tomorrow? How can we avoid learning situations that produce waste? How can we avoid social assumptions of inferiority that channel (and thus waste) potentially capable people? How can we control selectivity and modification that result in incorrect transmission of cultural behavior? How can we train people for the future?

The need for administrative decision makers, for instance, is increasing. How can we teach this kind of knowledge? Bateson suggests that we must be prepared to present in some fashion a readiness to use unknown ways to solve unknown problems. Jules Henry makes a similar comment: " . . . the capacity to rise spontaneously to the management of a new problem is again a capacity to be learned."[12] In some way we must master techniques to present, directly or indirectly, skills that enable our youth to be aware of relationships, even though elements of the situation are strange to them. As individuals learn only what is presented to them, the school system is responsible, as the major transmitter of sanctioned social behavior, to select and present the kind of behavior needed for adaptation to a changing cultural milieu.

In the final analysis, what is presented depends not only on the elements in the cultural base, but on who is available to present these elements. The *who* is, therefore, a crucial figure responsible for selecting, modifying, and interpreting cultural content. He also establishes the affective quality of the learning situation. He may serve as a model with whom the learner identifies, or an image whom he rejects.

---

[12] Jules Henry, quoted in John Honigman, *Culture and Personality* (New York: Harper & Row, Publishers, 1954), p. 138.

Chapter 5

Who Presents Cultural Behavior?

Major Concepts

Status   Role   Donor

Every individual during the course of his lifetime is assigned certain statuses by his fellows and, more or less effectively, practices behavior expected of him in associated roles. He neither learns nor participates in the entire range of cultural activities of his society. His participation is limited to a particular set of statuses and roles appropriate to his "place." This place is imputed to him by others with whom he interacts. His placement in a set of statuses may be biologically limited or socially determined. More often than not, however, social factors predominate.

Status is based on the socially recognizable characteristics of an individual, whether biological or learned, empirically observable or imputed to him by others. *Role* denotes the action patterns expected of anyone who lives up to that status. It involves inter-related practices—rights and privileges as well as obligations and duties associated with the status. Normally, such roles are played with varying skills.

Thus, the status of teacher has certain eligibility requirements that involve both explicit and implicit duties and obligations while guaranteeing certain privileges. Role expectations include certain standards of dress, age, previous training, classroom etiquette, colleague relationships, student relationships, and so on. Some expectations involve the manner in which the individual playing the role will interact with others; some designate characteristics of the individual which make him eligible to perform the role. The sum total of these expectations is understood, explicitly and implicitly, to be required if one has the status of a teacher. Obviously, some teachers fulfill one aspect of the requirements better than others.

All social situations are entered into with some understanding of role requirements—mutual expectations of participating individuals. Awareness of status conveys these role expectations; such knowledge usually precedes interaction, which is set in motion by status cognition. The Balinese, for instance, exercise care in seating themselves at any formal gathering—even young children are taught on which level to sit. Seating arrangements are determined by a hierarchy of rank; those of highest rank sit on the highest pavilion. A Balinese might well ask, "Where do you sit?" The reply alerts the questioner to the other's status and expected patterns of interaction. Thus, improper interaction is forestalled. Here, a similar question, though differently phrased, is asked at weddings: "Are you a friend of the bride or the groom?" The answer establishes not only role expectations but seating arrangements.

In a rapidly changing culture, new statuses and roles come into being. With the advent of the airplane, the status of pilot emerged and individuals learned the role; with space travel came astronauts, with the atomic age, atomic physicists, and so on. Such emerging statuses and roles are adjusted to existing relationships, and the "right" of the role player is sanctioned by the group. Status requirements and role expectations then become part of the cultural tradition; succeeding generations of individuals are taught, in one manner or another, the new aspect of culture.

The term *donor* refers to any individual who presents hitherto unknown behavior patterns to another. Such innovative behavior encompasses all acts that are new from the standpoint of the one who learns to perform them.[13] In the final analysis, all individuals are potential donors; new forms of behavior are transmitted continually to others. Such random transmission, however, is not under consideration at the moment. Rather, concern is directed to innovative behavior that takes on normative aspects and donor roles that are institutionalized. As observed, varying statuses involve differing eligibility requirements and role expectations. Ideally, only a qualified individual is accorded certain kinds of status, and once assigned to a status, others acknowledge one's right to perform the accompanying role. With mutual assumptions of this "right," "correct" social interaction is possible.

Among the privileges and obligations of many roles are mutual expectations of donor rights—the right to present specified kinds of behavior to others. When the "right" is standardized and culturally transmitted as part of the role expectation, it is termed a *donor* role. The role of the chief of the Tikopia people (Polynesia) is such a role; implicit in it is the right of final arbitrator on any matter. The chief may strike another, but because of his station none may retaliate. In our society, teachers play such a role, with the assigned right to present approved cultural material in standardized, formalized situations. In other parts of the world, the "teacher" may require no formal structure. Other well-known donors are clergymen (religious behavior), policemen (coercive behavior), and revenue officers (tax regulations).

Activities of the institutionalized donor are reinforced by others who create and maintain the conditions under which he functions. The teacher, for instance, is supported by a vast network of interacting individuals—administrative, political, economic, maintenance—who control the context, and as much as possible, the content of what is presented in the classroom. Thus the teacher, by virtue of fulfilling age and other social requirements, occupies this status and plays the appropriate role. This donor role is reinforced and controlled by our "school system;" Americans generally accept the teacher's right to teach specified cultural material.

---

[13] With apologies to Margaret Mead, the basis for this definition of "innovation" comes from her *Continuities in Cultural Evolution,* p. 85.

Who Presents Cultural Behavior?

All societies, on the basis of biological or social criteria, differentiate between members to a greater or lesser degree. Differentiation classifies people in varying age, sex, occupational, religious, ethnic, class, and caste groups, to name a few. This differentiation limits participation and determines who may present and learn cultural behavior.

In our society, sub-cultural groups are composed of individuals who, having learned cultural alternatives, may teach them; thus goals and values are held in common. Such groups also include donors whose personalities and teachings are acceptable and sanctioned within the group, but not necessarily by the society as a whole. Second-generation welfare children, for instance, may learn from their parents how to "live" on welfare—i.e., what they are "entitled to" from various governmental agencies. They often know the facts better than does the social worker. Usually they learn no other way of life, and their particular goals and values, unique to themselves, are at odds with taxpayers' beliefs.

It can be generally stated that a plurality of sub-cultural groups increases the number and kinds of donors presenting alternative ways of life. The possibility of conflicting presentation in a homogeneous society is much smaller. In non-literate societies, for instance, much behavior is presented within the family; often the extended family may represent the total society. Kin members bring individual behavior into line with the specific requirements of the culture. Explicit knowledge (skills) and implicit values (ideas and attitudes) are alike for all. Although major enculturation is a family responsibility, formal schooling at the hands of specialists is not ruled out.

In parts of Africa, "schools" require intensive courses of instruction, and long periods of seclusion for the learner. The Bavenda send their sons to school at the age of eight or nine. Reaching puberty, the young student is instructed in such techniques of warfare as ambush, night attack, and spying. Young men are also taught to make mats which must be finished within a prescribed period of time. Rules of etiquette are carefully presented. The deviant is severely punished by beating. "They emerge from their training hardened and disciplined, ready to shoulder the responsibilities as well as to share the privileges of a fighting man of the tribe."[14] Thus less complex societies throughout the world present behavior that is consistent in value orientation and insures cultural continuity whether it is accomplished within the family group or by specialists.

The Venda girls, on the other hand, attend school for only six days and nights; this period marks their passage from childhood to adolescence. They are taught tribal rules of etiquette and obedience, dancing, and sexual behavior. A mixed school brings both sexes together to instruct them in behavior expected of them when they marry, to point out the significance of the marriage step, and to warn them of possible problems that may develop during their lifetime.[15]

Specialization in any society increases the number of donor roles; the greater the division of labor, the greater the variety of donors needed to present alternatives of behavior to oncoming individuals. In our society, from early childhood we are aware of donor activity. We continually encounter different people presenting special behavior. Sunday school teachers, "gym" teachers, school teachers—"math," English, history, and so on. No one person could possibly present all we need know to adapt to our culture. Consequently, we look for presentation of knowledge by many donors, and are not surprised to find that another has been added to the list. There are even times when we are not certain who is responsible for presenting what, e.g., commercials: movie actresses present technical medical facts, actors teach integration, long-haired brunettes with guitars present foreign policy. Too often, we discover pragmatically that individuals presenting one or another kind of behavior do not have a right to do so—as the old story about the country "hick" who thinks he has bought the Brooklyn Bridge indicates.

Although biological factors may actually determine who may present behavior, more often supposedly biological restrictions are socially initiated. For instance, women were formerly considered incapable of learning medical skills, for assumedly biological reasons (innate ability). Actually, the criteria were social; this occupation was not considered "proper" for women. Of

---

[14] Herskovits, *Cultural Anthropology,* p. 187.
[15] *Ibid.*

course, innate ability and physiological capability do set limits on participation. A mentally deficient person could not teach higher mathematics; a ten year old does not normally cope with atomic physics, and a "golden ager" seldom presents acrobatics. In other words, "The physical structure and organization of each human organism determines the limits; the physical maturity and the amount of prior learning determines the rate . . . Each level of development varies greatly in different cultures."[16]

It is recognized, nonetheless, that some sex restriction on participation is universal; all peoples differentiate between women's work and men's work. In our society, however, sex-based restrictions upon presentation of cultural forms are virtually nonexistent. Elsewhere, such restrictions may be quite marked. In Africa, for instance, young unmarried girls do not present sex facts to peers; this right belongs to mature women. Women may be responsible for agriculture, and may teach and be taught these skills; men may do likewise in other areas. Women may form the spearhead of an army as do the women archers of Dahomey, or serve as religious mediators as do the Noro of Ryūkū. In former times in Java, only men taught in the Moslem schools; today, a few women are allowed to present religious instruction.

Just as sex may restrict the right to participate, so too does age. Donor rights may either increase or decrease with age. Old men in Samoa lose the right to rule. Our society defines us as old at 65, and withdraws our right to participate in many activities. The Eskimo, useless to the group as he grows old, leaves it to die alone. In other instances, the aged may be venerated, respected and heeded for his wisdom. Even "middle age" brings a loss of rights; it is not unusual for parents to lose instructional contact with their children at an early age—parents can tell them nothing. This inability to communicate with one's children is not universally common. The Rādjpūt child (India) usually seeks help only from adults who can provide more reward than can peers. It may be pertinent that Rādjpūt child-rearing practices do not encourage cooperation between children, as we do, for adults do not urge their young to comply with the requests of those in their age group

---

[16] Walter Goldschmidt, *Exploring the Ways of Mankind* (New York: Holt, Rinehart and Winston, Inc., 1960), p. 181.

or turn to help them in case of need. Nurturant behavior is not usual in the "teen-age" child.[17]

The Rādjpūts carefully spell out other "age rights." The oldest man, for instance, retains considerable authority and customarily disciplines male children of the family. A man, however, does not discipline his eldest daughter; such matters are in the hands of women. If he believes his wife is not strict enough, he will beat her. Discipline does not always lie in the hands of the adults but becomes the "age right" of the older children in some areas. Among the Samoans, a young "guardian" normally disciplines her small charge and is at all times responsible for her behavior. Knowing this, a young child often takes advantage of her guardian, for a scene brings punishment to the older child.

Few societies allow women to raise male children after a specified age, usually relatively young. Our society, however, allows the mother unlimited control over both male and female children; undoubtedly this situation greatly influences male personality structure. Even in matrilineal systems (descent through the female line), where the father has few rights over his children, the mother's brother controls the boys' activities. Among the Menangkabau of Sumatra, the maternal uncle is the key figure. This is also the case with the Bush Negroes of Suriname. The father may be responsible for providing food and shelter, but the uncle controls the boys' movements. A father would not consider taking his son canoeing, for instance, without permission of the mother's brother.

This custom is also practiced among the Tlingit-speaking peoples along the coastal zone of southeast Alaska. The mother's brother has prior rights, and teaches virtues, and warns against vices. In earlier days it is said that the uncle woke his nephew at daybreak and directed him to a nearby river (breaking the ice if necessary) to immerse himself until told to leave. All this was intended to make the boy strong, tough and full of courage. This insured that " . . . the house of the mother's father's father would not die out."[18]

---

[17] John Hitchcock and Leigh Minturn, "The Rādjpūts of Khalapur, India," in *Six Cultures,* Beatrice Whiting, ed. (New York: John Wiley & Sons, Inc., 1963), pp. 207-361.

[18] Ronald L. Olson, "Channeling of Character in Tlingit Society," in Douglas Haring, *Personal Character and Cultural Milieu* (Syracuse: Syracuse University Press, 1956), pp. 674-87.

It is perhaps of interest that some societies do not present certain kinds of behavior that we consider crucial. The Kaska Indians (Yukon Territory and British Columbia) do not train their members in any way for leadership. The Kaska is unaccustomed and unwilling to respond to a leader; no one has authority over anyone but his son. The development of strong, self-assertive individuals is discouraged; the aggressive are deviant.[19]

Our painstaking conceptualization of materials for teaching has a polar counterpart in other cultures, where no attempt is made to teach certain skills. The Kaska do not "teach" a young girl domestic skills. A child must learn by imitating the behavior of the adults; no explanation is given, for instance, to a small child told to "make tea." Left to herself, she might place the tea leaves in cold water and no one would take the trouble to explain that hot water was required for steeping.[20]

Margaret Mead has observed that " . . . one of the blocks in our failure to transform our present-day culture is our failure to recognize the extent to which different individuals, different occupations, classes and cultures depend on implicit learning from artifacts, on empathetic, imitative and identificatory learning, and on Gestalt learning—learning without intervention of a teacher."[21] This aspect is considered more fully in a later section.

Our analysis of *who* presents cultural behavior is not complete without consideration of the donor as a model with whom the learners identify. Often the manner of presentation is duplicated by the learner. Watching a number of student practice teachers "perform" in a classroom, the author was struck by the similarity of their activities to a certain member of the college staff. The tonal quality, sarcasm, shaming, and ridiculing of their students were so like their professor's that the individual herself might have been speaking. (Incidentally, the model was a very "bad teacher.") The professor had served as a model; imitative learning was obvious, and as the model was admired—identificatory learning (Freud called it introjection) occurred as well, to be perpetuated generation after generation.

---

[19] John Honigman, *Culture and Personality* (New York: Harper & Row, Publishers, 1954), p. 9.
[20] *Ibid.*
[21] Mead, *Continuities in Cultural Evolution,* p. 137.

One further aspect of donor rights and cultural roles is the reinforcement received universally from symbols: accouterments, titles, language usage or other sensory phenomena. The symbol acts as an alert to interacting individuals. In our society, for instance, the white coat of the medical doctor prepares us for all kinds of painful interaction that we certainly never would permit from one garbed otherwise. The cleric's collar, the policeman's uniform (as well as the turning, flashing red light on his car), the captain's bars, the chef's hat are but a few of the familiar identification symbols.

Americans presenting innovative behavior in various parts of the world are faced with the problem of understanding the significance of identification symbols. John Embree tells of the U.S. military government in a Micronesian Island issuing 100 pairs of navy greens, a kind of work trouser, to natives who looked "needy." The "needy" were widows, orphans, and people with no pants. Some time later, the chief of the tribe wore a pair of these pants to the administrative building. The executive officer, feeling that the chief did not qualify as "needy" reprimanded him. The chief was shocked at this attitude. What the Americans had failed to realize was the significance attached to the trousers by the islanders. Trousers were not items of need, but items of prestige in dress—a symbol of rank.[22]

Hogbin also tells of administrative problems in New Guinea after the war. Some of the local chiefs, having lost respect in their position because of failure to be just and honorable, were removed from office. The navy-blue peaked cap with a single broad red band was removed from one chief's head and burned ceremoniously—dramatic indication of the loss of "right" to rule.[23]

The introduction of a title (symbol of rank) into a social situation often determines or alters the pattern of interaction and establishes donor rights. Titles used in the academic hierarchy communicate to students the period of time they must wait for a late instructor; they also alert the administration to salary range. An early philosopher in China established careful definitions of kin terminology—"names" for each member of the extended kin sys-

---

[22] John Embree, "American Military Government" in M. Fortes, *Social Structure* (Oxford: Clarendon Press, 1963), pp. 207-23.

[23] H. Ian Hogbin, "Government Chiefs in New Guinea," in Fortes, *op. cit.*, pp. 189-206.

tem. Knowing a name of a kin thus meant understanding " . . . the exact position of a particular category of individuals in the social structure, and of knowing the rights and obligations which went with this position."[24]

Language usage also indicates who is eligible to present certain kinds of behavior. The use of distinctive jargon or colloquialisms prepares us for the users' rights. Communication virtually stops between colleagues of different disciplines, yet the words immediately alert the listener to the other's role. The Air Force publishes a wordy dictionary of terminology commonly used by its members. It is distinctively Air Force and quite incomprehensible to the outsider.

Thus, throughout the world, symbols of one kind or another designate those individuals who have the right to play a donor role. Role expectations and identifying symbols are transmitted culturally and people accept behavior from individuals whom these sanction. A factor hindering adult education is the adult's failure to acknowledge as many donors as the young. It also appears that adults are more exacting in establishing the donor's right to present. Erasmus, for instance, notes that in Haiti " . . . adolescents and young adults are far more receptive to new practices introduced by government agronomists than are the mature adults . . . since he (the young adult) apparently finds it easier to substitute the prestige of the specialist for the prestige of tradition."[25]

Interculturally, young men from "foreign" countries trained in the United States return to their homes to find their donor rights challenged. Elders of their society see in new cultural forms a threat to their own prestige and feel the conflict of men with traditional values. With the future apparently bringing prospects of a lifelong process to keep abreast of changing conditions, an understanding of the "credentialing" process is most essential. *Who* is acknowledged by various age, occupational, religious and ethnic groups (and so on) as having the *right* to present cultural prescriptives and alternatives.

---

[24] Ralph Linton, *Tree of Culture* (New York: Alfred A. Knopf, Inc., 1961), p. 546.

[25] C. J. Erasmus, "Agricultural Changes in Haiti," *Human Organization,* XI (1952), pp. 20-26.

Chapter 6

Who Learns Cultural Behavior?

Who presents and *who* learns cultural behavior are virtually opposite sides of the same coin; hence, similar concepts are employed in their analysis. As noted, normal individuals are expected to learn cultural prescriptives, i.e., language, kinship terminology, literacy in our society, and so on. Cultural alternatives, on the other hand, are selectively taught and learned. As is the case in presenting behavior, both biological and social factors limit or restrict the kinds of behavior in which learners participate. In any society, an individual's status is the criterion used by others to allow participation.

Biologically considered, the right to learn certain kinds of behavior is mainly a matter of sex and age differentiation. Among all peoples, the clustering of beliefs, values and sentiments around the matter of sex sometimes designates one sex as superior to the other, and sometimes excludes one sex from certain spheres of activity. Most groups try to rationalize these restrictions in terms of physiological differences between the sexes, e.g., their different roles in reproduction. However, a comparative study of statuses accorded to women and men in different cultures seems to show that while such factors may have served as a starting point for the development of diversification, the actual ascriptions are almost entirely determined by tradition. In societies where such restrictions are established, however, it is not uncommon for a girl to learn by imitation what a boy has been taught purposefully. An Eskimo woman, for instance, in an emergency may build an igloo, or an Ojibwa woman may hunt for game.[26] A bobby pin, in the hands of an American woman, has repaired many an electrical appliance.

Nevertheless, in many societies men learn the heaviest physical tasks, as well as those that require constant attention, great mobility, or emergency action. They apparently assume that women must take time out for childbearing or for monthly privacy where menstruation is surrounded with social restraints in the form of isolation or taboos. The predominance of men in political and military roles may be due to this factor. There is, however, some possibility that the phenomenon may be a species characteristic; male dominance may be related to the different hormone balance of males and females. It is also widely characteristic of mammals.

The exclusion of women from politics is very widespread. Even in matrilineal societies where descent and inheritance follow the female line, political control is in the hands of men, usually the maternal uncle. The Aranda of Australia virtually exclude women from all ceremonial, religious, and governmental matters. The Toda of southern India allow only men to learn the techniques and ceremonies connected with the care of cattle. Each class of dairy with its herds is tended by a special class of dairymen—the priests of the Toda.[27]

Age also is a factor determining who may learn. All societies open learning channels at certain points in the individual's life. Cross-culturally three broad categories are recognized: child, adult, and aged. However, biological passage from childhood to adulthood, and adulthood to aged does not always coincide with social transfer. Margaret Mead points out that many peoples tra-

---

[26] Mead, *Continuities in Cultural Evolution*, p. 63

[27] G. P. Murdock, *Our Primitive Contemporaries* (New York: The Macmillan Company, 1935), p. 39.

ditionalize cultural patterns that allow a child to learn when he is biologically *ready*. Other societies anticipate readiness and hurry the new generation into cultural behavior deemed essential or of particular value. Still others find participation in certain activities undesirable; they delay transferring knowledge long after the period of biological readiness.[28] Thus, various cultures sanction different maturation points; readiness is culturally defined.

Where skills are needed for survival, as in the Eskimo society, children are urged to learn and master the important techniques of survival at a very early age (five or six). In our society, at this same age a child is expected to have a well developed awareness of right and wrong. Among the Balinese, artistic and theatrical abilities are of great importance, and young children are urged to develop them. Skill in dancing, for instance, is so valued that very young children undergo intensive training. Mature dancers manipulate the child's arms, legs, head, and hands into the correct positions before he is actually capable of doing so himself. The skills of survival, which is much less precarious in Bali than among the Eskimo, are more casually learned. In Japan and other Asian countries, parents and teachers manipulate the child's hand in teaching writing and other skills.

The Arapesh of New Guinea give boy children small replicas of adult weapons to familiarize them with later duties. Bows and arrows are used to shoot small game, especially rats. In our society, it is rather ironic that the most popular "toys" are war tanks, guns and battleships. Arapesh children accompany their parents and participate in adult activities that require little skill. No particular emphasis is placed on perfecting skills; there seems to be, rather, an attempt to "ease" children into competency—to establish a pleasant identification with adult activities. Children are eager to learn adult behavior as yet barred to them. Among the Cheyenne, children learned to "live" by practice. A group of children camped out together with small tepees, weapons and so on. Plains Indians tell of a group that survived when the entire adult population was wiped out by a war party. Allegedly, some years later they were found living as adults, replicating the way of life of the parents.[29]

---

[28] Mead, *Continuities in Cultural Evolution,* p. 63.
[29] *Ibid.,* 64.

Our school system delays some aspects of learning and hurries children into others. Formal schooling is started at an early age (often children in other cultures have not yet been weaned); conformity, rationality, and literary skills are demanded well in advance of most societies. But we tend to underestimate the capability of many pupils by imposing alleged attention spans: first grade, twenty minutes, second grade, thirty minutes, and so on. Precisely how far concentration is biologically based, and how much is due to cultural expectations is debatable. Recent developments in technology, especially of warfare, most certainly have changed cultural expectations of learning pace. Accelerated learning in all grades has resulted.

Postponement of learning also is widespread. In our society, children are in a dependent position long after they are phsysiologically capable of adulthood. Social adulthood is nowhere clearly defined, and our youth are admitted to this level in a most haphazard fashion. Access to military activity is allowed at 18; political activity (voting) is delayed to 21; social maturity (drinking for instance) is determined by the State, while working privileges are withheld until after the age one's great-grandfather treked West with wife and child. In other cultures, such as the Arapesh, children are discouraged from crawling until they have cut their teeth. In Bali, because crawling is considered culturally undesirable, children are not urged to crawl and normally walk without previously crawling.

Casualness in expectations of learning is observed among many peoples. A Rādjpūt child is neither encouraged nor discouraged to crawl. If one should crawl, he is moved out of the way. When ready to walk, he does so. Talking is treated equally casually, and a child is considered unteachable until he has learned to speak. As soon as a child is able to walk and say a few words, demands will be made upon him. Failure to respond at this time to directions may bring punishment, although parents do not normally reason with their children or explain demands.

Among the Hopi, children begin to practice dance steps when they can barely walk. By age four, they have learned singing and drumming and begin to participate in such ceremonials as the Snake and Buffalo dances. There is no well defined area between work and play; the child spends his time in one or the other of these activities. By the age of ten, the child must have learned the fundamentals of the kinship system, the Hopi way of life and proficiency in social and economic duties; he must have become a productive and useful member of the society.[30]

In general, societies consider many activities appropriate only for adult learning, and children of either sex are forbidden access to this kind of knowledge. The Cheyenne, for instance, do not allow children near the Shaman's tent; the Samoan child may not go near the ceremonial council. In our society, adults tend to separate children from tragic situations and to withhold sex learning until after adolescence. This situation may be typical in cultures that separate the sexes in the bath, in sleeping quarters of the unmarried and so on. With puberty, some of these channels of learning are opened. In New Guinea, for instance, adolescent boys are taught ceremonial secrets from which they hitherto have been barred. At this time, the Arapesh explain the "supernatural" noises—drums, whistles, flutes, and so on—as natural phenomenon produced by uncles, older brothers and fathers. After learning ceremonial rituals, youth are expected to keep the secrets from the women and younger brothers. (This is much like Santa Claus in our own society.)

Among non-literate peoples such limitation of knowledge of the supernatural to adults is a common practice. Herskovits suggests that "The control of the powers of the universe is conceived as essential to the successful solution of their problems. But children, whose physical power is slight, are rarely conceded any great amount of spiritual power. Therefore, not until they become older are they taught the theological concepts and the ritual concepts of their tribe."[31] As a matter of fact, children in our society are barred from certain aspects of religion until certain age specifications are fulfilled.

Adulthood brings new learning, and in the United States, much for which we are not prepared. Assumption of adult status necessitates learning such new roles as sanctioned sex behavior, learning to live with a mate, organizing a family, living within a budget,

---

[30] Laura Thompson and Alice Joseph, "The Education of the Hopi Child," in Walter Goldschmidt, *Exploring the Ways of Mankind,* p. 191.

[31] Herskovits, *Cultural Anthropology,* p. 190.

holding a job. One of the tragedies of our society is the failure to present this behavior either directly or indirectly to many of our youth.

Just as certain learning comes with adulthood, so old age brings new learning requirement, for learning does not stop with achievement of adult status. In non-literate societies, both men and women are fitted to carry on their culture at an earlier age than in a literate, rapidly changing culture. The Comanche warrior did not prepare himself for old age, thinking it better to be killed in action. The Eskimo, useless and unproductive in old age, may leave the igloo to die alone in a storm. The Mesakin of East Africa must learn certain ceremonial duties assigned to the old men; the learning is frustrating and old age is resented. The Samoans as well resent the approach of age, as loss of the right to rule accompanies it.

Not everywhere, however, does old age bring resentment and loss of rights. Among the Chaga (Tanganyika Territory) grandparents have the responsibility of rearing at least the firstborn of their sons' children. In areas where ancestors are believed to be in control of the fate of the living, as in China, the aged continue to be respected and age increases their control over family members, for with death they will be very powerful individuals.[32] In our society, older men and women must learn leisure time activities, hobbies, and so on. Women must learn not to look old. LaBarre paints a rather depressing picture of American grandmothers, bobby-socked, girlish hairdos, and "... smearing onto their sagging jowls the greases and the colored dirts of synthetic youth."[33]

All social systems also limit or restrain learning on the basis of social criteria such as heritage, wealth, bravery, religious affiliation, education, occupation, devaluation of certain biological characteristics, and so on. Learning channels, for instance, are opened to some individuals because of kin relationships. Metal working skills (iron making) in Africa and Asia fall into this category. The distinct processes applied to particular ore-bearing rocks before they can be transformed into different material, which

---

[32] Herskovits, *op. cit.*, p. 584.

[33] Weston LaBarre, "Social Cynosure and Social Structure," in Haring, *Personal Character and Cultural Milieu* (Syracuse, New York: Syracuse University Press, 1956), pp. 535–46.

must then be heated and shaped into efficient tools, are techniques not likely to be invented more than once, and are believed to be magic. Possession of this knowledge is frequently kept in the hands of family guilds, whose power is believed to come from the supernatural controls they exercise, quite as much as from their technological knowledge.[34] Similar restrictions of knowledge to a family group can be found among the California Indian basket makers or South Sea Island canoe builders.[35]

In some instances, specialized learning is restricted to an entire tribe; a group in Melanesia, for instance, may manufacture pots and exchange them for another group's fishing nets. The caste system in pre-colonial India was normally a hereditary monopoly of a certain activity or occupation; learning the skills of a particular caste was limited to individuals related by birth. A complex interchange of goods and services was thus essential to the functioning of the Indian social system. In fact, the religious system of India bars all outsiders; a Hindu is born, not converted.

Limitation of occupational skills to families or special groups of people is not peculiar to non-literate peoples. Labor unions, for years, have barred members of certain ethnic groups from membership, thus making it virtually impossible for such individuals to learn trade "secrets." The late Earl Bell observed that ". . . there seems to be a universal tendency for class systems to develop caste-like characteristics . . . passing on wealth through inheritance and preventing the dissipation of inherited wealth through establishment of trust funds. . . . The Plumbers' Union controls the training program so rigidly that it is exceedingly difficult for one who is not the son of a plumber to get the necessary training. It is claimed that other things being equal sons of physicians are given preference in admission to many medical schools."[36]

An erroneous concept of innate racial inadequacy closes channels of learning to many American Negroes who are not allowed access to cultural alternatives that would give them greater advantages. Entertainment and athletics are in fact virtually the

---

[34] Herskovits, *Cultural Anthropology,* p. 142.
[35] *Ibid.,* p. 149.
[36] Earl Bell, *Social Foundations of Human Behavior* (New York: Harper & Row, Publishers, 1961), p. 382.

only channels sanctioned by the total society. Ethnic minorities are also barred from many alternatives. Medical schools, for instance, have imposed quotas to restrict the number of Jews admitted.

In pre-war Britain, commoners were barred from occupations controlled by the aristocracy; industry bars individuals with advanced degrees from menial positions. In feudal Europe, a man born into the peasant class could anticipate a life of tilling the soil, with little opportunity to learn other behavior. People knew their "place" and did not seek learning outside it.

Our school system continually opens channels of learning to some individuals and closes others to them on the basis of a battery of tests. Allison Davis has commented that "In making the linguistic factor the chief basis for judging mental capacity, the test makers have chosen one of the poorest indicators of basic differences in problem-solving capacity."[37]

One further phenomenon requires attention: the channel of learning that appears to be open to all, but, in fact, is not. Such a situation is brought to our attention by Margaret Mead in her discussion of the vision behavior of the Omaha Indians. Mead believes this cultural practice a ". . . carefully guarded method of ensuring the inheritance within certain families of membership in a medicine society."[38]

The Omaha tribe have a powerful group of religious practitioners, the Mide Society. Because of the prestige of these men, young adults were eager to gain membership. To qualify, one had to fast in the wilderness and have a "proper" vision. This vision must satisfy the elders of the society of the youths' right to membership. Unfortunately, many who aspired to this status were unable to have a vision that the elders considered authentic. A descritpion of an "authentic" vision was never made known; thus, final decision of what constituted a true vision always lay in the hands of a few. An authentic "vision" thus subjectively determined is a familiar experience to all of us: the Phd committee, "making the team," "If you work hard, you will be successful," and so on. We open channels of learning to many people who, in the final analysis,

---

[37] Allison Davis, *Social-Class Influences upon Learning* (Cambridge, Massachusetts: Harvard University Press, 1948), p. 85.

[38] Mead, *Continuities in Cultural Evolution*, p. 130.

will not be considered eligible for the final goal; certain implicit qualifications will remain unfilled, i.e., religious affiliation, color, accent, home address and so on.

Such "minority" discrimination retards the growth of the national income and deprives our society of potentially competent manpower. Thus, valuable human resources are wasted through a failure to allow development or utilization of skills. Just as one needs to examine prescriptive and alternative categories of material to be taught or withheld, so should he pay attention to arbitrary restrictions upon the presentation of some kinds of learning to special groups of people. In any society, it is essential to consider the extent to which important kinds of learning may be inaccessible to certain types of persons and to note the possible dysgenic effects upon the whole society in consequence.

Chapter 7

What Is Learned?

Major Concepts

Acculturation   Direct Learning
Enculturation   Indirect Learning
Modal Personality

Acculturation

Acculturation implies a particular kind of cultural transmission; two culturally distinct groups come together in time and place. Acculturation is said to occur when such contact is characterized by a fairly continuous interchange of implicit and explicit elements of culture. "Overseas" Americans, in frequent contact with peoples throughout the world, both teach and learn cultural practices. Dance forms, clothing, artifacts, and ideas are presented to others, while we, in turn, accept and practice some of the host country's customs. The American Indian as well as immigrating ethnic groups, while learning the "American" way of life, contributed to the formation of new American culture. Because of this acculturation process our social heritage today is diverse and varied.

Enculturation

Enculturation is also a process, the learning of a particular culture; learning begins with birth and continues until death. In this manner, all human beings learn to adjust to their particular cultural milieu. The individual's behavior is shaped and molded, either directly or indirectly, into patterned responses. This chapter is concerned with what is learned—that is, the enculturation process.

Direct and Indirect Learning

Human beings must learn, each generation afresh, the major portion of their behavior, especially those activities that involve symbolic communication. Thus, the mechanisms of learning are central in the functioning of all normal individuals. Essential in all learning, perhaps central therein, is control over and inhibition of random motions, and repeated selection of some specific routine of behavior. This may involve training of muscles to perform any task competently, disciplining impulses, acquiring thinking skills, and so on.[39] All learning—all acquisition of skills, thinking or overt, is possible only by continual inhibition of the fanciful and random aspects of behavior. Inhibition of inappropriate behavior should be understood as the price of learning.

Such learning may be acquired either directly or indirectly. Direct learning refers to the intended transmission of specific content—the substance of what is taught or acquired. Indirect learning involves acquisition of social behavior that is a by-product of the direct learning situation, or learning acquired by imitation, empathy or absorption (as when a child models his behavior after that of another whom he consistently observes). For instance, in a classroom a child learns directly that two and two make four. He may learn indirectly how to be a teacher; years later, he may

---

[39] Douglas Haring, *Personal Communication*. 1966. Bibliography V lists further readings in the general area of culture and personality.

bring into a teaching situation the same general attitudes to which he was exposed. Or again, a mother may teach her daughter (directly) to make a cake. After several attempts, only failures result. Despite parental efforts, the child has indirectly learned inadequacy.

Modal Personality

Whereas psychologists have stressed the uniqueness of the "person," cultural anthropologists have drawn attention to common elements or personality traits the "person" has in common with other members of his cultural community. Character traits that are representative and appear most frequently in a social group, are conceived of as "modal;" thus arises the modal personality. Similar personalities develop from experiences these individuals have in common; similar experiences in any given culture or subculture tend to produce similar personality configurations in individuals subjected to them. As what is learned or experienced varies from one culture to another, different modal personalities emerge, each shaped by cultural experiences.

As social experiences begin shaping personality virtually at birth, "culture and personality" specialists have amassed data to show that the techniques members of any society employ in the care and rearing of their young are instrumental in personality formation. Child rearing practices tend to be similar, though not identical within any specific culture; a child's experiences are relatively consistent with those of his age mates in his community; thus, he develops a personality like those of his peers. However, similar persons are not solely products of child rearing practices; social pressures brought to bear upon an individual throughout his lifetime continue, by means of rewards and punishments, to affect his personality. Personality is said to be a product of nature and nurture; modal personality is a product of similar nurture in many families or social situations.

What Is Learned?

To speak to an educator of learning is rather like carrying coals to Newcastle; one may always hope, however, one of the lumps of coal may be a diamond. Generally speaking, any normal human given motivation and opportunity, may in time learn what is presented to him; what a man of one "race" or culture has learned, another may learn as well. As a species, man has an encompassing capacity to learn and an ability to think symbolically. What he does learn rests, in the final analysis, on what is presented, directly or indirectly, i.e., what he has access to socially.

What is learned directly is not necessarily identical with what is presented. Accuracy of transmission is influenced by such factors as the learner's previous experience or training, awareness of the various elements of the learning situation, symbolic orientation, and so on. Though human social behavior is learned from contact with other human beings whose cultural practices are relatively uniform, our society brings into contact groups of individuals with respective sub-cultural similarities that differ considerably from each other.

Thus our integrated and regional school system, for instance, brings together different kinds of children from varying cultural backgrounds. Such groupings, though highly desirable in terms of our prescriptive values—democracy, equality and brotherhood— widen the gulf between what is presented and what is learned. This is probably not so evident in the case of overt behavior that may be continually observed and checked for accuracy. However, covert behavior (ideas, concepts, attitudes) is completely dependent on symbolic communication, and subject to a high degree of modification even under the best of circumstances.

In essence, all cultural behavior is symbolic; words, body motions, artifacts, marriage, religion, and all human social interaction depend on the understanding of symbols. Language is only one part of our symbolic system. Children from different classes or sub-cultural groups attach different meanings to concepts. In addition, language defines the experiences that an individual may have. There is a tendency to project unconsciously the implications of any word into the field of experience. For instance, if your vocabulary includes a word that expresses "kindness" and no word for "unkindness," social relations are conceived in terms of degrees of "kindness," or of one or another form of kindness.

First grade readers once included stories of Farmer Brown and his farm animals, far removed from the urban dweller who reads only words. Much was conveyed, however, to the farm boy who "saw" in the words all his experiences with the types of cows (for instance) or one particular cow. This personal experience with cows lasted as part of his growing awareness through his lifetime. The urban child continued to see "cow" in flat perspective, although many other happenings were very real to him.

The different interpretation students may attach to words came sharply to the author's attention not too long ago. At one point in my teaching career, it became necessary to use the term "instrumental" (referring to instrumental leadership). I did not bother to define the word, assuming that all present understood it. Blank faces soon alerted me to the fact that this was far from the case. At least three different meanings were proposed: violin, dentist's drill, and "of God." Luckily for this later telling, each child came from the family background that the reader already may have assumed: musical, medical, and ministerial.

What is learned is also influenced by the learner's awareness of the total learning situation. Few individuals enter any situation aware of all its aspects—implications, innuendos, meanings and so on. Consider the "parlor" game in which numerous articles are placed on a table; people file by, seat themselves, and write the name of every object they can remember. Some, of course, remember more than others; many individuals are not aware of having seen certain items that were in plain view. When a situation is comprised of covert, symbolic "objects," total awareness is virtually impossible. The degree of awareness is a product of previous experience and training. Becker suggests that Madison Avenue is sensitized to subtle differences in cigarette filters—far more so than other consumers.[40] Painters are aware of colors a non-painter does not see. Thus a serious discussion on painting would convey a message in depth to a painter, a superficial communication to a non-painter, and no message at all to a color blind individual.

In any class room, a teacher may present selected course content; this material is selectively modified by each pupil. The amount of modification is determined by the degree to which the learner's background resembles that of the teacher's. Sub-cultural experiences and linguistic symbolism in common would tend to

---

[40] Ernest Becker, *The Birth and Death of Meaning* (New York: The Free Press of Glencoe, 1962), p. 15.

increase "faithful" transmission of content. The wider the divergence between the two backgrounds, the less possibility that an accurate message is learned.

As noted, people cannot behave socially in ways that have not been learned. Yet often, it is expected that they do so. Many high schools, for instance, still present as prescriptive, literary works by such authors as Hawthorne, Dickens, and Shakespeare, virtually excluding recent publications. Although books from the past are indeed essential to liberal education, such traditional training is little help to college-bound seniors if patterns of writing and expression best suited to college requirements are not learned.

At one time, the school curriculum was reinforced, by indirect learning experiences outside the classroom. Extensive reading "taught" one the "feel" of correct English. Reading has been replaced, to a great extent, by continual viewing habits. However, television and other mass communication utterances may or may not be "good" English, and their vocabulary is limited. This may be the case also in peer and family groups. Within the classroom, increasing numbers of teachers from "middle-class," first- and second-generation American homes speak an English greatly colored by their home setting. Thus, directly, students are presented an English that is no longer part of present-day cultural milieu, and indirectly, the average student receives little reinforcement of direct training. Thus, although he is expected to produce "well written" material in college, the average student receives minimum contact with a clear and understandable written English.

Ruth Benedict discusses an instance of this phenomenon that we might term "expectation without presentation." In 1953, she introduced the concept of discontinuous learning and its secondary effects on personality development. Often, early learning is not directly relevant to adult expectations. The American society, for instance, restricts the adolescent from sexual behavior and often even discussion about sex. Later, the individual is expected to forget connotations of "wrong" associated with all sexual behavior, and adjust satisfactorily in the marriage role—a kind of behavior that is unlearned. The secondary effects lie in the fear of such adult roles. Benedict comments ". . . it is not surprising that in such a society many individuals fear to use behavior which has up to that time been under ban and trust instead, though at great psychic cost, to attitudes that have been exercised with approval during their formative years."[41]

A fear of adult roles apparently existed in Manus. Mead found in 1928 that the Manus children looked on adult life with ". . . loathing, with a sense that life was filled with heavy restrictions and hard work, exploitation by financial entrepreneurs or heavy, unending economic responsibility as entrepreneurs themselves."[42] By 1953, when she revisited the area, she found the children participating in adult activities with pleasure. She concluded that earlier the children were identifying with the adult's deep rejection of the adult role. Cultural change, in the interim, had eliminated many of the "grueling exchanges" common under the old system and adults at this later date were enjoying their activities.

"Culture and personality" specialists have repeatedly emphasized the importance of indirect learning in personality development. Kardiner, for instance, states "There is a limit to the sort of culture content which can be transmitted by direct learning process . . . ;" that direct transmission cannot account for "the integrative character of the human mind in so far as the emotional relationships of the individual to his environment is concerned."[43] Mead emphasized the great importance, in all societies, of empathetic, imitative, identificatory, and Gestalt learning.[44] Thus, a concluding probe is directed into *what is learned* indirectly in various cultures. Such a question is best approached by examining several studies of child rearing practices.

Behavior resulting from indirect learning permeates all our actions, many of which are incorrectly assumed to be instinctive. LaBarre, in studying emotions and gestures, found that many had a cultural basis and were not instinctive human gestures.[45] He

[41] Ruth Benedict, "Continuities and Discontinuities in Cultural Conditioning," in Kluckhohn and Murray, *Personality in Nature, Society, and Culture* (New York: Alfred A. Knopf, Inc., 1948).

[42] Mead, *Continuities in Cultural Evolution*, p. 60.

[43] Abram Kardiner, "The Concept of Basic Personality Structure as an Operational Tool in the Social Sciences," in *Personal Character and Cultural Milieu*. Haring.

[44] Mead, *Continuities in Cultural Evolution*, p. 137.

[45] Weston, LaBarre, "The Cultural Basis of Emotions and Gestures," in Haring, *op. cit.*

discovered, for instance, that the simple act gesturing "yes" or "no" was culturally determined. As we nod our head to express "yes," and shake it to signify "no," other peoples differently convey this meaning. The Semang of the Malay Peninsula, for instance, thrust the head sharply forward for "yes" and cast down the eyes for "no." Some Indians visiting this country through the "Experiment in International Living" consistently indicated "no" by nodding the head. This proved extremely disconcerting to the American group interacting with them, as a "no" message was being received as "yes." The Ainu of northern Japan do not use head movements, but the right hand passed back and forth, chest high, indicates "no," and the raising and lowering of both hands, palms upward, to the chest signifies "yes." The Dyaks of Borneo raise their eyebrows to mean "yes," and contract them to express the opposite.

LaBarre observes that sticking out the tongue, used by Europeans to express contempt for another, is differently interpreted elsewhere. In Bengali, the tongue often protrudes in this fashion in statues of the mother goddess, Kali, to signify rage, anger, and shock.[46] The Tasmanians stamp their feet rapidly on the ground to express surprise or pleasure, while an American expresses anger with the same behavior. In village Thailand, a woman may stamp two or three times on the floor as soon as a baby is born, so the child will not be frightened by later noises.

Even walking is culturally shaped. The precise gait of the well-trained military man is distinctive, as is the gait of the men who "ride the range." Missionaries in Burma claim they can distinguish between the Shans and the hill people by their gait, even though they are dressed in the same kind of garment. The hill people ". . . keep time to each step by swinging the arms from side to side in front of the body in semi-circular movements, but the Shans swing their arms in a straight line and do not bring the arms in front of the body."[47] A more familiar example is one contributed by Sapir—the peculiarly East European Jewish gait that is a kind of shuffle or trudge, ". . . lost by the very first generation brought up in this country."[48]

---

[46] *Ibid.*
[47] *Ibid.*
[48] *Ibid.*

Although formal schooling, with direct transmission of knowledge in this fashion, is not a factor in the education of the young of most non-literate societies, there is no lack of educational techniques to encourage, to discipline, to punish. Overt training by elders, imitation of the behavior of older children, observation of the mature at ceremonies or at daily tasks, are all educational techniques used by non-literate peoples. These same processes are at work in literate societies. Because observation of others' cultures tends to be more objective than study of our own, the study of child rearing practices in less complex societies has proven of infinite value in understanding the interplay of direct and indirect learning in the formation of personality.

In her study of the Alorese, Cora DuBois contributes to this growing body of knowledge.[49] Attention is focused on the relationship between adult anxiety over food, a basic physiological drive, and child rearing practices and disciplines, as well as the extension of this anxiety into other institutionalized behavior. DuBois distinguishes three types of discipline: permissive, restrictive, and absorptive. Permissive discipline encourages the child, by means of a reward system, to acquire certain behavior. Restrictive discipline, by punishment (either physical or withdrawal of approval) denies the child certain types of activity. Absorptive discipline is not consciously imparted; behavior is so consistently observed that the child makes it part of his own normative behavior.

The Alorese child is cared for constantly by the mother for about six days after his birth; by the end of the tenth day, as the main provider of the family, the mother returns to the gardens. Unlike many societies where women are the agriculturists, the Alorese does not carry the baby with her, but leaves him to the ministrations of the father or older sibling. Apparently, this care is spasmodic and uncertain, for the baby is hungry far more often than he is satisfied. Thus, even during infancy, gratification of hunger is a disappointing experience. When the baby walks, he is left to his own devices; no one is apparently responsible for his care. No one is concerned with his crying protest. Often the child

---

[49] Cora DuBois, "Attitudes Toward Food and Hunger in Alor," in Haring, *Personal Character and Cultural Milieu, passim.*

lives only on bits of food from early morning to late afternoon, when his mother returns from the fields.

Any skills the child may acquire during the first two or three years of life are the result of absorptive or restrictive learning. In the first instance, he models his behavior after those around him who have made no conscious attempt to "teach" him. In the second case, he soon becomes aware of the futility of protesting against hunger and neglect.

DuBois observes that the inconsistent and restrictive quality of discipline surrounding this child might well be expected to foster a sense of insecurity and suspicious distrust. Seeing only one way, crying and rage, to gain his own ends, he soon learns that even this approach is not particularly effective. The alternate idea, of being good to gain what is wanted, never is presented to the child. He has learned indirectly to depend on his own resources; very early in life he forages for himself in others' gardens; he "steals" what he needs to satisfy his hunger.

One can easily anticipate the adults' attitude toward food; there is little generosity in distributing it. Although an occasional guest may be fed, any indication of "free-loading" cancels the possibility of a second invitation. The fear of theft especially from the gardens, is great. Consequently, curses against theft are erected in the fields to protect the crops. These curses, made by experts, are bamboo poles with magical objects inserted into a cleft top. It is believed that these curses inflict some fatal disease on any thief who ventures into the field. Other, possibly cautious people, keep guards around the fields to fine or shoot thieves.

The close identification of the child with the mother—the only individual who conscientiously cares for him—apparently establishes the wife as a "mother figure." She, like the mother, is a provider. Older men often lecture young people after a quarrel by telling the girl she should be as a mother to her husband, the young man, as a father to his wife.

DuBois concludes that a child who has learned that the gratification of hunger is a precarious and uncertain thing may well become an adult who shows obsessive attitudes toward the waste of food. This is especially so, she feels, if he sees adults continually anxious over this matter. She considers the whole pattern of training among the Alorese to be restrictive (punishment ranges from physical violence to withdrawal of approval); no training is permissive. All the child's experiences are reinforced by daily absorption of adult behavior oriented around anxiety over food.

Honigman made a similar study of the Kaska Indians of the Yukon Territory.[50] Interested in the enculturation process, he studied how child-rearing practices shape a kind of people best fitted to live in the Kaska society. The Kaska men are trappers and hunters, often alone and traveling long distances to maintain a trap line. Women remain at home, caring for the children, trapping small game and waiting for the men to return. The infant receives prompt attention from the mother who assumes most of the responsibility for his care. As the baby grows older, he receives constant attention, although adults show little interest in promoting the child's development. Honigman observes, for instance, that he seldom saw a child held upright to encourage him to walk. Nevertheless, people show concern if any expected sequence of maturation fails to appear. Weaning is a slow process, completed by the age of three; at this time the mother, the primary source of affection, withdraws from the child. More remote and less receptive to his demands, she apparently becomes less concerned with his welfare. Crying is ignored. Persistent demands may be met with a sharp reprimand. Soon the child learns not to run to his mother, and relies on himself.

Children are carefully guided away from aggressive behavior; a show of anger, quarreling or antagonistic acts are considered extremely undesirable. With the exception of these controls, boys receive little instruction until adolescence when they accompany older brothers or a maternal uncle on the trap line. Girls accept responsibility at an earlier age, six or seven. Education is casual, unplanned and mainly indirect (absorptive). The child learns by observing or imitating the adults' behavior. No explanation of the task is given. Repeated failures may or may not bring advice.

The adult Kaska Indian, independent and unaccustomed to leadership, is unwilling to respond to a leader. He feels responsible for his own success or failure. Unaggressive, he avoids situations that give rise to anger. Honigman observes that outbursts are infrequent. All strong emotion is supressed; affection lies between

---

[50] Honigman, *Culture and Personality*, pp. 3-10.

parents and children, husband and wife. In fact, The Kaska, emotionally isolated, has acquired an adult personality quite congruent with his political and interpersonal interdependence or atomism.

Six Cultures, edited by Beatrice Whiting, contains several excellent studies of child-rearing practices. Minturn and Hitchcock depict the life of the Rādjpūts of Khalapur of India.[51] The authors indicate that the center of life for these agricultural people is in the courtyard where women and children spend most of their time. Women in the household are usually wives of brothers, their younger children, their unmarried daughters, married sons' wives and so on. In other words, this is an extended family system with two or three generations related by blood in the male line.

Among the Rādjpūts, sons are greatly preferred to daughters, for family prestige depends largely on wealth and manpower. Boys are potential farm help and bearers of the family lineage. Girls, on the other hand, are an expense as they require a sizeable dowry. There is a high infant mortality rate and the health of the newborn infant is a matter of anxiety to the parents. Many magical customs have grown up around this concern. Supernatural dangers and spirits are believed responsible for illness; ghosts may make children ill, or possess them.

All babies sleep with their mothers for several years. Girls may continue this practice longer than the boys who join the men on the "men's platform." During the day, the baby is left in the courtyard in an out-of-the-way place. He is completely covered with a cloth, which keeps the insects away, and also hides the child from envious glances. It is believed that the evil eye may be put on a child by someone who is jealous of him. A child is never complimented, as this not only draws attention to him, but puts also the praiser in the suspicious position of "throwing the evil eye." When not demanding attention, the child is ignored. He is not diapered; neither feeding nor toilet training are compulsive. Children are not urged to eat if they are not hungry. The necessary daily bath, however, is firmly rejected by the young baby. With

[51] John Hitchcock and Leigh Minturn. "The Rādjpūts of Khalapur, India," in *Six Cultures,* B. Whiting, ed. (New York: John Wiley & Sons, Inc., 1963), pp. 203-362.

this exception, his life is free of stress. Babies are viewed as members of a group rather than as individuals. They are objects of neither particular interest nor great concern: "All children are alike."

The baby spends his first two years as a passive observer in the courtyard. Although never alone, he is never the center of attention. When ready to walk, he does; he is neither encouraged nor discouraged to do so. Until he can speak, he is considered unteachable; no one expects any modification of his behavior. Only when he has command of the language is he considered capable of learning from verbal instruction.

Specific individuals are responsible for disciplining the child. For instance, no other woman, not even the mother-in-law, punishes a child if his own mother is near and has seen him misbehave. Among the men, discipline is normally in the hands of the eldest. A father would leave disciplinary action to him. A man does not discipline his daughters; this is left to the women. Normally discipline takes the form of ridicule or scolding. Fear of rejection by the group seems to be a powerful motive for conformity. Children are not threatened with the wrath of gods or ancestors for misbehavior; evidently this is considered improper. Nor does a parent punish children by withholding rewards (the mother has few tangible rewards to offer). Food is never withheld as a disciplinary technique, as refusal to accept food is rather common—a culturally patterned way of expressing displeasure. Children seldom receive praise, which is believed to spoil them and make them disobedient.

The apparent lack of sibling rivalry seems the result of three factors. Adults, never overly affectionate with any of the children, give none special attention. As no child is ever the center of attention, he never is displaced by another. In an extended family system, women always are available to care for the child, even if the mother is busy with a new baby. Furthermore, it would be unusual for a child to have the status of first-born in such a household. Other babies are always there—children of older uncles, uncles of his own age and so on. The child is a secure but unimportant member of the group.

Since children are believed to learn from observations, the Rādjpūts make little attempt to reason, explain or instruct a child. Failure to accomplish a task may bring scolding; such scolding,

however, does not include a description of how the work should
have been done. The authors believe that "all socialization techniques employed by the adults are probably less effective in the
modification of the children's behavior than the observation and
imitation through which the children gradually absorb the skills,
customs, and values of their group . . . The children learn from observation.[52]

The adult Samoan expects no privacy, remains relatively de-
tached in all interpersonal relations, and is extremely unintense,
and unaggressive. One may well ask how he became this kind of
person. What process of enculturation is practiced by the Samoans?
The answer is found in *Coming of Age in Samoa,* by Margaret
Mead.[53]

The Samoan baby is fed whenever he cries. As soon as he is
able to hold his head erect, he rides everywhere on his young
guardian's hip. The young baby sleeps with his mother until
weaned and then is transferred to the care of an older sister. Responsible for the child's behavior, she often "gives in to him" to
prevent a scene that brings her a scolding. Neither the child's
first words or steps are met with any degree of attention.

Children continue to sleep in the same room with adults, and
are not separated from events like birth and sexual intercourse of
the parents. This casual treatment of the children prevents the
development of compulsive attitudes. Children are not restricted
to their own household, and are welcomed by any relative in the
village. A girl may wander from house to house, staying wherever
the food is best and the scolding least. Children are welcomed for
their contribution to the working force.

A girl, particularly, is taught neither to try too hard (for she
must avoid any reputation of precociousness), nor to be lazy
(this would decrease her opportunities for marriage). Thus, the
Samoan way of life provides little chance for privacy; people are
taught not to seek it. A Samoan learns not to be noticed. Children
are discouraged from asserting themselves and must not presume
beyond their age. The practice of living with one relative after

---

[52] *Ibid.,* p. 331.
[53] Margaret Mead, *Coming of Age in Samoa* (New York: William Morrow
Co., Inc., 1950).

another restricts the development of strong ties with any one person. The Samoan, too, reaches adulthood a product of enculturation and adjusted to the expectations of his society.

The complexity of our society increases the difficulty of isolating the channels of indirect learning. In the last war, Gregory Bateson researched the psychological implications of Nazi propaganda films and the manner in which these films shaped German attitudes toward the Nazi Party.[54] He contends that these films did not present propaganda in isolated utterances but presented " . . . themes built into the structure of the plot in such a way that the audience, while enjoying the plot . . . necessarily accept the underlying themes as basic premises, which may never be articulately stated." Underlying themes, he contends, were expertly woven into a pro-Nazi background and tied to family life. The plot is so structured that the audience is unwittingly encouraged to accept the basic premise that ideology is related to family structure.

Students in an introductory anthropology class conducted a recent study of the "Culture of Cheating"—at what age it began and how it was transmitted. The students found that a major goal of pre-first grade teachers was to present attitudes of cooperation, and to foster cooperative behavior. All behavior termed "cooperative" was identified and described. Observation of first and second grade behavior indicated that the pupils had indeed learned cooperation. Unfortunately, however, much of what had been learned was later re-classified as "cheating."

In the course of the study, one student reported an attempt by the teacher to impress upon her class that work now must be completed individually. Preparing to give a test, she cautioned the class, "Each do your own work," and added, "Now tell me if you see anyone copying." Some time later, a small boy raised his hand and declared, "Mary is copying." The teacher's reply was for him to attend to his work; she gave no word of reprimand for Mary. All in the class had learned a lesson: one is not really expected to report instances of cheating.

It is beyond the scope of this paper to treat indirect learning in this society. Not enough research has been done by anthropol-

---

[54] Gregory Bateson, "Cultural and Thematic Analysis of Fictional Films," in Haring *Personal Character and Cultural Milieu,* p. 137–43.

ogists in identifying our channels of indirect learning. Yet this kind of learning molds a major part of each American's personality. It is hoped this may be an area of inquiry for anthropologists and educators to explore together.

Chapter 8

Conclusion

Thus the anthropologist, whether physical, cultural, archaeologist, or linguist, focuses his attention on man, his works, and his cultural behavior. The cultural anthropologist is associated perhaps more closely with the field of education, for, in its broadest usage, education is the transmission of both implicit and explicit cultural behavior to members of a society. In a narrower sense, our formal school system is a cultural phenomenon.

In any society, individuals are both creators and recipients of education. Thus, the author has considered the part they play in the enculturation process. Individuals who fulfill certain culturally defined eligibility requirements present behavioral patterns to other arbitrarily designated persons, who directly and indirectly learn, select and modify parts of the presented content.

In our society, the school system directly presents a major part of our cultural prescriptives and alternatives. The portion learned indirectly is immeasurable. To identify and control indirectly learned behavior is probably impossible, perhaps undesirable.

Yet diversity of behavior resulting from sub-cultural experiences precludes the possibility of a well integrated society.

The responsibility of counteracting this influence rests with our school system. In some manner, teachers must present behavior to increase the behavioral experiences that the young have together; the more behavior that can be presented in common, the more effectively the young will be able to adjust to their environment and to each other for the rest of their lives. In the final analysis, the major goal of education is to give young and old alike habits and patterns of behavior by which they may live.

Glossary

ACCULTURATION: the modification of a culture through more or less continuous contact with another.

ACHIEVED STATUS: a social position open to elective struggle.

AFFECTIVE: pertaining to emotional facets of behavior.

ASCRIBED STATUS: a fixed social position not open to competition, e.g., sex or age.

CASTE: a class whose status is ascribed, i.e., with no competition, endogamous.

CHARACTER: the distinctive qualities of a society or a person.

CLASS: a grouping of persons who feel a common unity and a sense of distinctiveness from other groupings.

COGNITIVE: pertaining to knowledge or ideational facets of behavior.

CONFIGURATION: a dominant or unifying tendency within some larger whole.

COVERT: not accessible to observation, hence inferred (e.g., thought processes).

CULTURE: the totality of learned, socially transmitted behavior.

DIFFUSION: the spread of an element from one cultural system to another.

DONOR: an individual who presents innovative behavior.

ENCULTURATION: the process of learning a cultural tradition.

ETHNIC GROUP: a group with more or less distinctive culture.

EVOLUTIONISM: the search for general laws of cultural growth; more strictly, a theory of unilinear development.

EXTENDED FAMILY: a family group consisting of several closely related nuclear families.

FORM: an observed regularity, as in objects, ideas, actions.

FUNCTION: the relation of an element within some larger whole.

HIERARCHY: a relationship involving higher and lower rank.

HISTORICALISM: the study of specific cultural elements in time and space.

INCEST: to mate within a forbidden degree of close kinship.

INNOVATIVE BEHAVIOR: all acts that are new from the standpoint of the one who performs them.

INSTITUTION: an established form of behavior.

INTERACTION: the interrelations of individuals in a social group; the play of interpersonal relations.

MODAL PERSONALITY: the central or dominant personality characteristics more or less shared by all members of an ethnic group.

NEOLITHIC: pertaining to the New Stone Age.

NORM: the expected or ideal tendency, e.g., of behavior.

PALEOLITHIC: pertaining to the Old Stone Age.

PATTERN: a regularity, e.g., of behavior.

PERSONALITY: the characteristics of the individual, particularly those resulting from learning and training.

PRESCRIPTIVE: required, e.g., marriage rules.

"RITES DE PASSAGE": rituals connected with crisis or "passing over" points in the individual life cycle.

ROLE: the part played by an individual or group expressive of status.

SANCTION: a validating and enforcing mechanism.

SET: a direction or tendency, as with a dominant characteristic giving integration to a culture, or a pattern of interaction among individuals.

SHAMAN: an individual religious expert.

SOCIALIZATION: the process of becoming a member of society.

SOCIETY: the aggregation of individuals in an organized group.

STATUS: a social position.

STIMULUS DIFFUSION: the stimulation of creativity in one culture through contact with elements of another culture.

STRUCTURE: a regularity of form.

SYMBOL: a form or fixed sensory signal to which some permanent meaning is arbitrarily assigned.

TRAIT: a minimum significant unit of culture.

TRAIT-COMPLEX: an associated group of traits.

VALUE: an emotionally charged preference or standard of worth.

Bibliography

I.   Standard General Textbooks

Beals, R. L. and H. Hoijer. *An Introduction to Anthropology*. Third edition. New York: The Macmillan Company, 1965.

Boas, Franz, *et al. General Anthropology*. New York: D. C. Heath & Co., 1938.

Goldschmidt, Walter. *Exploring the Ways of Mankind*. New York: Holt, Rinehart and Winston, Inc., 1960.

Hammond, Peter. *Cultural and Social Anthropology*. New York: The Macmillan Company, 1964.

Herskovits, M. J. *Cultural Anthropology*. New York: Alfred A. Knopf, Inc., 1955.

Hoebel, E. A. *Anthropology: The Study of Man*. New York: McGraw-Hill Book Company, 1966.

Honigman, John. *The World of Man*. New York: Harper & Row, Publishers, 1959.

————. *Understanding Culture*. New York: Harper & Row, Publishers 1963.

Keesing, F. *Cultural Anthropology*. New York: Holt, Rinehart and Winston, Inc., 1966.

Kluckhohn, C. *Mirror for Man*. New York: Whittlesey House, 1949.

Kroeber, A. L. (ed.). *Anthropology Today*. Chicago: The University of Chicago Press, 1953.

Linton, Ralph. *The Study of Man*. New York: Appleton-Century, 1936.

––––––. *The Tree of Culture*. New York: Alfred A. Knopf, Inc., 1955.

Lowie, R. H. *An Introduction to Cultural Anthropology*. New York: Holt, Rinehart and Winston, Inc., 1940.

Mandelbaum, David G., Gabriel Lasker, and Ethel Albert (eds.). *The Teaching of Anthropology*. American Anthropological Association, Memoir #94, 1963. Note: see this for further reading suggestions and teaching methods.

Pelto, Pertti J. *The Study of Anthropology*. Columbus, Ohio: Charles E. Merrill Books, Inc., 1965. Consultant: George D. Spindler.

II.   Physical Anthropology

Boyd, N. C. *Genetics and the Races of Man: An Introduction to Modern Physical Anthropology*. Boston: Little, Brown & Co., 1950.

Coon, Carleton. *Origin of Races*. New York: Alfred A. Knopf, Inc., 1962.

Count, Earl. *This is Race*. New York: Schoman, 1950.

Cressman, L. S. "Western Prehistory in the Light of Carbon #14 Dating," *Southwestern Journal of Anthropology,* VII:3, 289-313.

Day, Michael. *Guide to Fossil Man*. London: University of London Press, 1966.

Dobzhansky, Theodosius. *Mankind Evolving*. New Haven: Yale University Press, 1962.

Hoebel, E. A. *Anthropology: The Study of Man*. Third Edition. New York: McGraw-Hill Book Company, 1966.

Howells, William. *Mankind in the Making*. Garden City, N. Y.: Double-day & Company, 1959.

Mandelbaum, D. A., *et al*. *The Teaching of Anthropology*. American Anthropological Association, memoir #94, 1963, 67-111.

Montagu, M. E. A. *An Introduction to Physical Anthropology*. Third edition. Springfield, Ill.: Charles C. Thomas, Publisher, 1960.

Pelto, Pertti J. *The Study of Anthropology*. Columbus, Ohio: Charles E. Merrill Books, Inc., 1965.

III.   Archaeology

Atkinson, R. J. C. *Field Archaeology*. London: Methuen, 1953.

Beyer, H. O. *Philippine and East Asian Archaeology and its Relation to the Origin of the Pacific Islands Population*. Manila: National Research Council of the Philippines, Bulletin 29, 1948.

Boule, M. and H. V. Vallois. *Fossil Men*. New York: Dryden Press, 1957.

Braidwood, R. J. *Prehistoric Men*. Sixth edition. Popular Series, The Chicago Natural History Museum, Anthropology no. 37, 1963.

Braidwood, R. J. and L. Braidwood. "The Earliest Village Communities in Southwestern Asia," *Journal of World History*, I, 1953, 278-310.

Breuil, H. *Four Hundred Centuries of Cave Art*. France: Centre d'études et de documentation Prehistoriques, 1952.

Childe, V. G. *What Happened in History*. New York: Penguin Books, 1946.

Clark, J. D. *World Pre-History: An Outline*. New York: Cambridge University Press, 1961.

Clark, J. D. and S. Piggot, *Prehistoric Societies*. New York: Alfred A. Knopf, Inc., 1965.

Daniel, G. E. *A Hundred Years of Archaeology.* London: Duckworth, 1950.

DeTerra, H. "New Evidence for the Antiquity of Early Man in Mexico," *Revista Mexicana de Estudios Anthropologicos,* VIII (1946) 69-88.

Fraser, Douglas (ed.). *The Many Faces of Primitive Art:* A Critical Anthology. Englewood Cliffs, N. J.: Prentice-Hall, Inc., 1966.

Heizer, R. F., *Archaeologist at Work.* New York: Harper & Row, Publishers, 1959.

————. *A Guide to Archaeological Field Methods,* Revised edition. Palo Alto, Calif.: National Press, 1958.

Mandelbaum, David, *et al. The Teaching of Anthropology.* American Anthropological Association, Memoir #94. 1963, 219-261.

Taylor, W. W. *A Study of Archaeology.* American Anthropological Association, Memoir #69, 1948.

Wheeler, M. *Archaeology from the Earth.* Oxford: Clarendon Press, 1956.

Willey, Gordon. *An Introduction to American Archaeology.* Englewood Cliffs, N.J.: Prentice-Hall, Inc., 1966.

Willey, G. R. (ed.). *Prehistoric Settlement Patterns in the New World.* New York: Viking Fund Publications in Anthropology, No. 23, 1956.

IV.   Linguistics

Anshen, R. N. *Language: An Inquiry into its Meanings and Functions.* New York: Science of Culture Series, Vol. III, 1957.

Birdwhistell, R. "Kinesics," *Explorations,* Vol. 4, 1955.

Bloomfield, Leonard. *Language.* New York: Holt, Rinehart and Winston, Inc., 1933.

————. *Language History from Language.* New York: Holt, Rinehart and Winston, Inc., 1965.

Carothers, J. C. "Culture, Psychiatry and the Written Word," *Psychiatry*, Vol. XXII, November, 1959.

Dei, L. Takeo. "Japanese Language as an Expression of Japanese Psychology," *Western Speech*. XX (1956) 90-96.

Graff, W. L. *Language and Languages.* New York: Russell & Russell, Publishers, 1964.

Hoijer, Harry (ed.). *Language in Culture.* Chicago: The University of Chicago Press, 1954.

Kallenbach, W. Warren and Harold M. Hodges. *Education and Society.* Columbus, Ohio: Charles E. Merrill Books, Inc., 1963.

Mandelbaum, David *et al. The Teaching of Anthropology.* American Anthropological Association, Memoir #94. 1963, 271-315.

McLuhan, Marshall. *The Gutenberg Galaxy.* Toronto: University of Toronto Press, 1962.

Sapir, E. *Language: Its Nature, Development and Origin.* New York: Harcourt Brace & World, 1921.

Smith, Alfred G. *Communication and Culture.* New York: Holt, Rinehart and Winston, Inc., 1966.

Whorf, B. L., *Language, Thought and Reality"* in *Selected Writings of B. L. Whorf,* J. B. Carroll, ed. New York: Technology Press of Mass. Inst. of Technology, 1956.

V. Cultural Anthropology

Ausubel, David. *Maori Youth.* New York: Holt, Rinehart and Winston, Inc., 1965.

Barnouw, V. *Culture and Personality.* Homewood, Ill. : Dorsey, 1963.

Bateson, G. *Naven.* Stanford, Calif.: Stanford University Press, 1936.

———. "Morale and National Character," in *Civilian Morale,* Watson, ed. Boston: Houghton-Mifflin Co., 1942.

——— and M. Mead. *Balinese Character.* New York: New York Academy of Sciences. Special Publication, 2., 1942.

Becker, Ernest. *The Birth and Death of Meaning.* New York: The Free Press of Glencoe, 1962.

Bell, Earl. *Social Foundations of Human Behavior.* New York: Harper & Row, Publishers, 1961.

Benedict, Ruth. *Patterns of Culture.* Boston: Houghton-Mifflin Co., 1934.

Brameld, Theodore. *Cultural Foundations of Education.* New York: Harper & Row, Publishers, 1957.

Doi, L. Takeo. "Some Thoughts on Helplessness and the Desire to be Loved," *Psychiatry,* XXVI, 1963.

DuBois, Cora. *The People of Alor.* Minneapolis, Minnesota: University of Minnesota Press, 1944.

———. "The Dominant Value Profile of American Culture," *American Anthropologist,* VII, 1955.

Erickson, Erik. *Childhood and Society.* Second Edition. New York: W. W. Norton & Co., Inc., 1963.

———. *Insight and Responsibility.* New York: W. W. Norton & Co., Inc., 1964.

Firth, R. "Authority and Public Opinion in Tikopia," in *Social Structure,* M. Fortes. London: Oxford University Press, 1949.

———. "Personality, and Language in Society," *Sociological Review,* XLII, (1950), 37-52.

———. "The Study of Values by Social Anthropologists," *Man,* LIII, 1953.

Fortes, M. *Social Structure*. Oxford: Clarendon Press, 1949.

Fraser, Thomas M. *Fisherman of South Thailand*. Ithaca, New York: Cornell University Press, 1966.

Hallowell, A. I. "Values, Acculturation, and Mental Health," *American Journal of Orthopsychiatry*, XX, 1950.

———. "Culture, Personality, and Society," in *Anthropology Today*, A. L. Kroeber, ed., Chicago: University of Chicago Press, 1953.

Haring, Douglas G., ed. *Personal Character and Cultural Milieu*. Syracuse, New York: Syracuse University Press, 1956.

Henry, Jules, *Jungle People*. New York: Vintage, 1964.

Herskovits, M. *Cultural Anthropology*. New York: Alfred A. Knopf, Inc., 1955.

Honigman, John. *Culture and Personality*. New York: Harper & Row Publishers, 1955.

Hsu, Francis L. K. *Psychological Anthropology*. Chicago: Dorsey Press, 1961.

Kardiner, Abraham. *The Individual and His Society*. New York: Columbia University Press, 1939.

Kluckhohn, Clyde. "Patterning as Exemplified in Navaho Culture," in *Language, Culture and Personality, Essays in Memory of Edward Sapir*, L. Spier *et al.*, Salt Lake City: University of Utah Press, 1960.

——— and H. A. Murray. *Personality in Nature, Society and Culture*. New York: Alfred A. Knopf, Inc., 1948.

———, Florence Kluckhohn, F. Strodtbeck and J. Roberts. *A Study of Value Orientations*. New York: Harper & Row Publishers, 1961.

Kneller, George F. *Educational Anthropology*. New York: John Wiley and Sons, Inc., 1965.

Landes, Ruth. *Culture in American Education.* New York: John Wiley and Sons, Inc., 1965.

Lee, Dorothy. "Freedom, Spontaneity and Limit in American Linguistic Usage," in *Explorations* IV (1955) 6-14.

———. *Freedom and Culture.* Engelwood Cliffs, New Jersey: Prentice-Hall, Inc., 1959.

Linton, Ralph. *The Cultural Background of Personality.* New York: Appleton-Century, 1945.

Mandelbaum, David. "On the Study of National Character." in *American Anthropologist,* V (1953) 2.

Mead, Margaret. *Coming of Age in Samoa.* New York: William Morrow, Co., Inc., 1961.

———. *Growing Up in New Guinea.* New York: New American Library, Mentor Books, 1930, reprinted 1953.

———. *Sex and Temperment in Three Primitive Societies,* New York: Mentor Books, 1950.

———. "Our Educational Emphases in Primitive Perspective," *American Journal of Sociology,* 48:6 (1943) 633-39.

———. "National Character", in *Anthropology Today,* A. L. Kroeber, ed.. Chicago: The University of Chicago Press, 1953.

———. *Continuities in Cultural Evolution.* New Haven: Yale University Press, 1964. See also this bibliography for other references on this general topic.

——— and M. Wolfenstein. *Childhood in Contemporary Cultures.* Chicago: The University of Chicago Press, 1955.

Minturn, Leigh and William Lambert (eds.). *Mothers of Six Cultures-Antecedents of Child Rearing.* New York: John Wiley, and Sons, Inc., 1964.

Murdock, George. *Primitive Contemporaries.* New York: The Macmillan Co., 1935.

Phillips, Herbert. *Thai Peasant Personality.* University of California. 1965.

Opler, Marvin. *Cultural and Mental Health.* New York: The Macmillan Company, 1959.

Smith, R. J. and K. Beardsley. *Japanese Culture: Its Development and Characteristics.* Viking Foundation Publications in Anthropology, No. 34, Parts III - IV, 1962.

Spindler, G. D. *Education and Anthropology.* Stanford, California: Stanford University Press, 1955.

————, et al. *Education in Culture: Anthropological Approaches.* New York: Holt, Rinehart and Winston, Inc., 1963.

Spiro, M. E. "Culture and Personality," *Psychiatry,* XIV, 1951.

Thompson, L. "Attitudes and Acculturation," *American Anthropologist;* Vol. L, 1948.

Wallace, Anthony. *Culture and Society.* New York: Random House, 1961.

Whiting, Beatrice (ed.). *Six Cultures.* New York: John Wiley and Sons, Inc., 1963.

Whiting, J. W. M. and I. L. Child. *Child Training and Personality: A Cross-Cultural Study.* New Haven: Yale University Press, 1953.

Index

7394   0